Achievement Motivation and Achievement in Mathematics

Achievement Motivation and Achievement in Mathematics

By
Mandalapu Srinivasa Rao
M.A., M.A., M.Ed., M.Phil., PGDCA, PGDDE
Department of Mathematics
A.P. Social Welfare Residential School
Pallapatla–522 262
Guntur, A.P., India

Editor
Dr. Digumarti Bhaskara Rao
M.Sc., M.A., M.A., M.Ed., Ph.D.
R.V.R. College of Education
D–43, S.V.N. Colony
Guntur–522 006
Andhra Pradesh

DISCOVERY PUBLISHING HOUSE
NEW DELHI-110002

Edition - 2015

ISBN: 978-81-7141-674-5

Achievement Motivation and Achievement in Mathematics

Published by:

DISCOVERY PUBLISHING HOUSE PVT. LTD.
4383/4B, Ansari Road, Darya Ganj
New Delhi-110 002 (India)
Phone: +91-11-23279245, 43596064-65
Fax: +91-11-23253475
E-mail: discoverypublishinghouse@gmail.com
sales@discoverypublishinggroup.com
web: www.discoverypublishinggroup.com

Printed at:
Infinity Imaging Systems
Delhi

Preface

Achievement motivation stands for the accomplishment of excellence and the achievement in mathematics stands for the performance of students in mathematics. As per the assumptions and research studies, one influences the other. A study, hence, has been undertaken to identify the level of achievement motivation and achievement in mathematics possessed by SC and OBC students studying in APSWR Schools and to study the association between achievement motivation and achievement in mathematics.

The students of APSWR Schools are possessing an average level of achievement motivation and achievement in mathematics. There is no association between achievement motivation and achievement in mathematics.

This study will be of great use to the policy planners, educational administrators and practising teachers in planning better curricular and Co-curricular programmes in schools.

Dr. Digumarti Bhaskara Rao

"Sai Soudha"

D-43, S.V.N. Colony

Guntur

Contents

1

Conceptual Framework

Overview

This chapter provides the conceptual framework of the study and thus serves as the introductory phase of the report. It consists of ten sections. The first one gives an overview of the entire chapter. The second furnishes the concept of education. The third section outlines the teaching-learning in mathematics. The fourth section gives an idea of the concept teaching in mathematics. The fifth section outlines the definitions of psychology and educational psychology. The sixth section furnishes the information about motivation. The seventh section gives an idea about achievement motivation. The eighth section briefly describes the evaluation and evaluation in mathematics. The ninth section furnishes the background of the study. The last one furnishes the documentary notes on the references cited in this chapter.

Education

The term 'education' does not have a definition of universal acceptance. There are numerous definitions of education and meanings that are suggested by these definitions. The origin of the word 'Education' is from the Latin root 'Educare'. 'Educare' means 'to lead out or to bring forth': it implies that through organised questions the knowledge, understanding and the potentialities of children have to be brought out; it is not pouring in knowledge assuming that children are like empty vessels.[1]

Gandhiji's definition of education in the Harijan issue of 1937, fits into the meaning implied here : "Education is drawing out of the best in child and man - body, mind and spirit."

Swami Vivekananda also has defined education in a similar way : "Education is the manifestation of the perfection that is already in man." It means that there is a 'self' in man which is self-contained and is a part of the universal reality.

Some other important definitions of education are given below.

"Creation of a sound mind in a sound body."— *Aristotle*

"Enabling the individual to be a producer as well as a good citizen."— *Nehru*

"Training the intellect, refinement of the heart and discipline of the spirit."— *Radha Krishnan*

"From the broad point of view, all life thought fully lived is education."— *William H. Kilpatrick* [2]

"Education is the development of all those capacities in the individual which will enable him to control his environment and fulfil his possibilities." — *John Dewey* [3]

By all the definitions of education, we conclude that, the meaning, functions and objectives of education may be explained as under.[4]

Educative Process

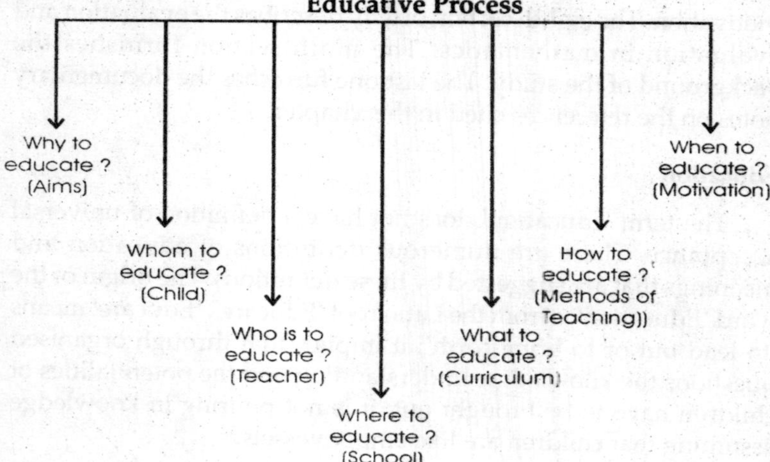

Why to educate?

This includes the aims of education. The educator and the educand must be clear about the aims of education so that efforts are made in the right direction. Aims of education depend upon a host of factors : political, economic, social, geographical, religious, etc. In a nutshell, education must produce socially efficient individuals.

Whom to Educate?

The educator must understand the educand thoroughly his aptitudes, interests, temperaments, etc., so that the 'best of him' is 'drawn out'.

Who is to Educate?

The teacher is to educate and he must thoroughly understand himself also. He must get rid himself off all the blemishes and remember "woe to the teacher who teaches one thing with the lips and carries another in the heart".

Where to Educate?

The child is to be educated in a school which must 'simplify', 'purify' and 'idealise' the environment.

What to Educate?

This leads to the contents of the curriculum which has been described as "the environment in motion". In a broader sense, it includes all the courses, readings, associations and activities that go in the school - in the classroom, library, laboratory, workshops, playgrounds - and in the numerous informal contacts between teachers and pupils.

How to Educate?

This involves the knowledge and technique of various methods of teaching for making the teaching-learning process dynamic, effective, and inspirational.

When to Educate?

This is concerned with the different stages of the child so that 'motivational' aspects may be handled and attended to psychologically.

Teaching-Learning

The purpose of teaching is to help pupils to learn. Each pupil learns, however, from his own efforts and experiences. A teacher may inspire a student to what to learn and may guide him in experiences from which he may learn some fact, attitude or skill, but the teacher cannot learn it for him. Each individual must learn for himself.

A good teacher can play important roles in the learning of an individual.[5] He can (1) observe the individual and try to understand his present abilities, interests and needs, (2) stimulate and encourage him to explore them further, and (3) help to provide further experiences of such a nature as he can probably use in satisfying the needs and curiosities he feels at the moment. The effective teacher is an artist at guiding a student's experiences in ways that will satisfy, atleast in part, some of the needs he feels at that time. What a particular individual actually learns from an experience may be quite different from the things his teacher had expected him to learn. The new knowledge or interest gained by a person through an experience is always an outgrowth of his previous concepts and interests, rather than the particular growth that the teacher had hoped the experience might stimulate.

Teaching and learning at the high school and college level are not essentially different in their fundamental nature and relationships from teaching and learning at the elementary school level. Older learners have usually developed, however, certain habits and abilities that were not strong in earlier years. Older children have usually learned, for example, to sit still for longer periods of time.

They have often learned to find certain kinds of information for themselves by turning to the dictionary or to other sources of information. Most of them have learned to depend more on themselves and less on what the teacher or text book say for finding satisfactory answers to the questions in their minds.

The most effective teachers, in high school and colleges as well as in the primary grades, are artists at recognizing, encouraging and developing the normal desires of young persons to understand and make intelligent use of the things that appear to concern them. An artist teacher can recognize and nourish a student's desire to develop more adequate understandings, even though the particular concern of the student at the moment may not be a part of the limited subject that the teacher was employed to teach.

Concept Teaching in Mathematics

"Any one can be a mathematician. Most people will not agree with me, I know. But, I insist that any person with average intelligence can master the science of mathematics with proper guidance and training."[6] — *Shakuntala Devi*

Mathematics is the mother of all sciences. The world cannot move an inch without mathematics. Every businessman, accountant, engineer, mechanic, farmer, scientist, shopkeeper, and even a street hawker requires a knowledge of mathematics in the day-to-day life.

Mathematical training is essential to children if they are to flourish effectively in the newly forming technological world. No longer it is enough to train children to meet known challenges, they must be prepared to face the unknown because it seems certain that tomorrow won't be much like today. It is now time for us to rethink our approach to mathematics learning.

The teaching of mathematics slightly differs from the teaching of other subjects in the point that, in the case of other subjects the child can make up the lost portion if he was absent at the time of teaching of that subject.[7] But this is not possible in mathematics, because it is a sequence subject. It is difficult to follow a topic when the topics that have been dealt with earlier are not properly understood. One cannot follow multiplication and division unless he knows addition and substraction. Simple interest, discount and stock cannot be understood unless one knows percentage. The parents and the teachers generally forget this fact. A boy deficient in this subject, if promoted to a higher class can only follow the course if he has made up his deficiency, which needs special coaching which few can afford and extra work on the part of the pupil. If at all the boy makes up his deficiency, the class by then has more further. Under the present system of school organisation, it is almost impossible to pay individual attention. The pupil cannot keep pace with the class, thus he is discouraged and neglected. Similarly, pupils irregular in attendance also fare no better. So, these two types of pupils remain backward in mathematics throughout their school career.

Mathematics is basic to a large number of branches of human knowledge. The habit of thinking can be developed through the study of mathematics. Study of mathematics is very much advocated in the educational programme for the development of higher order mental capacities like critical thinking and logical reasoning. One of the major aims of teaching mathematics is to create an enduring interest and faith in the subject and to develop a love for it.

To learn such a dynamic subject like mathematics, the student needs achievement motivation to acquire all the values and uses. Not only to learn mathematics but also to learn any subject, achievement motivation is the main factor.

In conclusion, we are cautiously optimistic about the potential for meaningful change in the teaching of mathematics.[8] The dramatic advances in technology will almost surely force change both in what mathematics is taught and in how it is taught. Research on learning and research on teaching are on the threshold of providing the kinds of knowledge that could lead to real advances in mathematics instruction. Change is inevitable. If we can build upon a solid knowledge base derived from research on teaching and learning, the change could result in real programme in the teaching and learning of mathematics.

Psychology—Educational Psychology

Psychology is the scientific study of behaviour and mental processes.[9] The term 'Psychology' comes from the Greek words

"Psyche" (the soul) and "logos" (study) and reveals the original definition as the study of the soul (later, of the mind). Scientific study implies using such tools as observation, description and experimental investigation to gather the information and then organizing this information. Behaviour is defined broadly to include actions that can be readily observed, such as physical activity and speaking, as well as other "mental processes" that occur even though they cannot be observed directly, such as perceiving, thinking, remembering and feeling.

Psychology is a systematic and consistent description and interpretation of behaviour with a view to control and predict it.[10] Facts of experience and behaviour are collected, classified and described and an attempt is made to interpret and explain them. All kinds of processes, activities, experiences, adjustments, responses to all kinds of life situations like thinking, feeling, remembering, perceiving, imagining, striving and acting are included in the study of psychology. Psychology deals with the whole field of living activity with all types of responses made by the living organism.

Educational psychology is a subject to be studied, an area or field of knowledge, a set of applications of laws and principles from a field of knowledge to a social process, a set of tools and techniques and a field for research.[11]

An educational psychologist is an applied psychologist. He is interested in the fundamental laws of human behaviour, but he is also interested in their applications to education.[12]

Educational psychology is an applied branch of psychology. It is psychology dealing with human behaviour in educational situations and is concerned with such facts and principles of human behaviour as faced within the scope of the social process of education.[13] Educational psychology should help the teacher to acquire a comprehensive approach to educational problems, to discriminate between remote and immediate goals of education, between impossible and practicable objectives and between suitable and unsuitable methods.

Motivation

In order to make learning in the subject meaningful, it is necessary that the students are motivated before they are made to learn anything.[14] A strong interest should be aroused and whole-hearted attention to the extent of concentration should be secured. Motivation is the basic activity for creating interest. Various means such as aids, relationships, historical references, anecdotes, possible applications, games can be adopted to provide motivation. Therefore, motivation is an essential condition of learning. Emphasizing the importance of motivation in the learning process, Kelley has stated that "Motivation is the central factor in the effective management of the process of learning. Some type of motivation must be present in all learning."[15]

Motivation, in its psychological sense, is concerned with the inculcation and stimulation of the learner's interest in the learning activities. It makes a student interested in his studies and a farmer in his farming. It is the force which energizes a man to act and to make constant efforts in order to satisfy his basic motives.

Tremendous research has been done on psychology of motivation in the last 50 years and a number of new theories have been evolved to explain human behaviour. K.B. Madson in his book "Theory of Motivation" has given twenty-four theories of motivation which propose different explanations of human behaviour. Historically, the word 'motivation' comes from the Latin root 'moveers' which means to move. Thus, we can say that, in its literal meaning, motivation is the process of arousing movement in the organisation. The movement is produced and regulated through the release of energy within the tissues.

The activating forces for the motivation may be termed as needs, drives or motives.[16] Needs are general wants or desires and are said to be the very basis of our behaviour. They can be broadly classified as biological and socio-psychological needs. Biological needs include all our bodily or organic needs such as the need for oxygen, food, water, rest, sleep, and sex and the like. They are linked with the survival of the organism and the species. Socio-psychological needs, like the need for love and affection, security, affiliation, self-assertion and self-actualization are linked with the socio-cultural environment and psychological make-up of an individual. They are considered essential as their deprivation may seriously affect the survival and welfare of an individual.

A need gives rise to a drive which activates an individual from within and directs his activities to a goal that may bring about the satisfaction of the need. Biological needs give birth to biological drives such as the hunger, thirst and sex drive, and socio-psychological needs produce socio-psychological drives such as the fear, anxiety, approval and achievement drives. Drives are also influenced and guided by incentives like praise, appreciation, reward, bonus, etc., as reinforcing agents.

What used to be understood by the word 'drive' has now-a-days been replaced by the more forceful term 'motive'. It is defined as an energetic force or tendency (learned or innate) working within the individual to compel, persuade or inspire him to act for the satisfaction of his basic needs or attainment of some specific purposes.

Psychologists have identified and named a number of motives. Hunger motive primarily arises from our body's need for food and the thirst motive from the need for fluid. The need for food or fluid is conveyed to the brain which inturn produces the motivation behaviour involving hunger or thirst. Apart from the biological function, the hunger and the thirst motives are also controlled by personal experiences and social learning. The sex motive, although not as essential for an individual's survival as food and water, constitutes a highly powerful psycho-physical motive. The maternal motive is stimulated both by biological factors and social learning.

Motives like the aggression motive, the affiliation motive and the achievement motive are purely learned as they are linked with the demands of one's environment in terms of social learning.

While curiosity can be considered as an immediate, autotelic motivation because it is immediately reinforcing and the reinforcement lies in the interaction between person and task (in uncertainty reduction), achievement motivation can be considered an extended person - intrinsic motivation because its reinforcement is delayed and arises from an interaction within the person. This motivation is a pattern of planning of actions and of feelings connected with striving to achieve some internalized standard of excellence, as contrasted, for example with power or friendship.[17]

Over time, the individual assesses his or her behaviour and evaluates the result. Achievement motivation is also called need for achievement (n-Ach). Important is the attitude to achieve rather than the achievements themselves.

The need to achieve appears to be a need that becomes part of an individual's personality and affects that person's behaviour in every facet of life including education. Individuals with a high need for achievement are people interested in excellence for its own sake rather than for the extrinsic rewards it can bring such as money or prestige. They prefer situations in which their personal responsibility affects the outcome. They tend to prefer to control their destinies and to make independent judgements based on their own evaluations and experience. They choose challenging goals (McClelland, 1958) and prefer delayed, larger rewards to immediate, smaller rewards.

Educationally, work is used for achievement and achievement has been sparse and only moderately successful. It was demonstrated that under some circumstances high need-for-achievement people will persist longer at a challenging task. Challenge, especially that of marks or grades in school, has been investigated; but since need-for-achievement is considered to be an intrinsic motivator and independent of external reinforces such as grades and prizes, it cannot be expected that there should be a high correlation between it and school achievement.

Since need-for-achievement is regarded as a learned motivation, training programmes have been developed for children to enhance their levels of it, and encouraging findings have demonstrated that even though academic grades may not have improved greatly, purposeful planning and action in many phases of life have resulted.

The conditions under which achievement motives best develop require that learners[18]

1. Can give reasons for developing a given motive.
2. Understand that the motive is realistic.
3. Can link the motive to deeds and daily events in life.
4. Commit themselves to concrete goals.
5. Keep a record of prospects.
6. Have honest and warm support.
7. Engage in self-study
8. Feel that they belong to a successful group.

Achievement Motivation

The need to achieve is the spring board of the achievement motive.[19] In a competitive society or set-up, the desire to excel over others or achieve a higher level than one's peers is intensified which inturn may lead to a stronger drive or motive to achieve something or everything that is essential to beat the others in the race and consequently experience a sense of pride and pleasure in the achievement. The type of motivation produced by such desire for achievement is called the achievement motivation, and has been defined in various ways. Some of such definitions are given below.

Atkinson and Feather—"The achievement motive is conceived as a latent disposition which is manifested in overt striving only when the individual perceives performance as instrumental to a sense of personal accomplishment."[20]

Irving Sarnoff—"Achievement motive is defined in terms of the way an individual orients himself towards objects or conditions that he does not possess. If he values those objects and conditions and he feels that he ought to possess them he may be regarded as having an achievement motive."[21]

McClelland and Atkinson - "Achievement motivation may be associated with a variety of goals, but in general the behaviour adopted will involve activity which is directed towards the attainment of some standard of excellence. Competition with others in which they are beaten may be included in it."[22]

From the above definitions, the achievement motive moves or drives an individual to strive to gain mastery of difficult and challenging situations or performances in the pursuit of excellence. It comes into the picture when an individual knows that his performance will be evaluated, that the consequence of his actions will lead either to success or failure and that good performance will produce a feeling of pride in accomplishment. The achievement motive may thus be considered to be a disposition to approach success or the capacity to take pride in accomplishment when success is achieved in an activity.

The theory of achievement motivation was developed by McClelland and his associates in 1951 at the University of Harward. According to him, human beings differ from one another in the strength of achievement motive. It is this difference in the strength of motivation to achieve that is important in understanding the differences in the economic growth of nations.

Development of achievement motive is affected by a number of variables in home, school and society.[23]

Home plays an important role in the early training of children for the development of attitudes and motives. Parental expectation and guidance to the child develop need for high achievement in life.

The society and its social philosophy is an important variable in developing achievement motive. There are communities which are achievement-oriented. There are other societies which believe in fate and leave every thing to God.

The child normally, now-a-days, enters school at a age of 4 years. Before coming to school, the child has gathered many experiences which become an integral part of his personality and form his attitude towards life, but even then the school can help a lot to sharpen already acquired experiences and develop positive attitudes in children. The teacher can play a very crucial role in the development of achievement motive by the following methods.

1. The teacher should make clear the importance of achievement motive in life by means of telling the stories

of great men and their achievements from all walks of life. When the students are convinced in advance to believe that they would or should develop achievement motive, the efforts of the teacher will succeed.

2. The teacher should provide a proper environment in the class and outside the class. The teacher's attitude and enthusiasm will create better environment for achievement motive in children.

3. The teacher will succeed in his attempt if he convinces the students that developing a new motive is realistic and reasonable.

4. The teacher should relate the motive with future life of the students and assign independent responsibility to them.

5. The teacher should make clear to the students that the new motive will improve their self-image.

6. The teacher should emphasize upon the fact that new motive is an improvement on prevailing cultural values.

7. The teacher should make students committed to achieving concrete goals in life related to the newly developed motive.

8. The teacher should ask the students to keep the record of their progress towards their goal.

9. Self-study should be emphasized.

10. The teacher should make an effort to develop conducive social climate in the class so that every individual should feel that he belongs to a group.

Achievement motivation is the expectancy of finding satisfaction in mastering challenging and difficult performances.[24] Achievement motivation is motivation to perform specific tasks for which there is a standard of excellence against which results can be judged.

Evaluation in Mathematics

C.E. Beeby (1977) described evaluation as "the systematic collection and interpretation of evidence leading, as part of the process, to a judgement of value with a view to action".[25]

There are four key elements in this definition. First, the use of the term systematic implies that what information is needed will be defined with some degree of precision and that efforts to secure such information will be planned. The second element, interpretation of evidence introduces a critical consideration, sometimes over looked in evaluation. The third element, judgement of value takes evaluation far beyond the level of more description of what is happening in an educational enterprise. The last element of Beeby's definition, with a view to action, introduces the distinction between an undertaking that results in a judgement of value with no specific reference to action and one that is deliberately undertaken for the sake of future action.

Evaluation is the heart of the educational process, for it helps to determine whether the goal of schooling, the expected and desired behaviour changes, have been attained.[26] Progress in learning can be recognized by observation but such casual observation is incomplete and inaccurate and may be erroneous. Evaluation must be done systematically, and student's performance, their status, growth and development in various areas of behaviour and personality must be correctly, comprehensively and methodically appraised.

The effectiveness of instruction is usually determined by measuring achievements against objectives undertaken.[27] An efficient programme of evaluation no longer comprises merely the effort to check the completed process but rather in the continual appraisal of the student's progress towards the attainment of pre-established aims. There is probably no more accurate barometer of the fundamental philosophy of any curriculum than a careful analysis of its evaluation programme.

The main purposes of the evaluation programme may be listed as follows:

1. To help provide more intelligent guidance in teaching and learning.
2. To develop more effective curricula and educative experiences.
3. To secure more intelligent and effective co-operation from parents and community.
4. To provide an adequate and objective basis for reporting progress.

Apparently, when most persons think of evaluation they think of tests. Some one hundred million standardized tests of the true-false, completion, matching or multiple-choice type are used each year and many millions of pupils are tested each year by locally constructed objective and essay examinations. If the numerous objectives[28] set by the schools are to be evaluated, however, teachers must use many procedures for evaluation other than tests.

Among the lists of most common objectives set by schools, one commonly finds such general headings as these :

1. The development of effective ways of thinking,
2. The cultivation of useful work habits and study skills,
3. The inculcation of constructive social attitudes,
4. The acquisition of a wide range of interests,
5. The development of increased appreciation of music, art, literature and other aesthetic experiences,
6. The development of social sensitivity,
7. The development of better personal social adjustment,
8. The development of skill in reading, writing, oral and aural phases of language,
9. The acquisition of important information,
10. The development of physical health, and
11. The development of consistent philosophy of life.

Evaluation of pupil's progress toward such objectives, with all their sub- divisions, is not possible by means of tests. Evaluation is a much broader and more complex process than the giving of tests.

For evaluating pupil's work we need definite measures. Accuracy in the measurement of school products should be used to improve the learning of children and the organisation of the school and to find out those students who need remedial teaching, especially tutoring or transfer to other work.[29] Examinations, as they are functioning, still dominate all levels of education. In teaching, evaluation is inevitable. It is this method that enables the teachers to know about the achievement of the students. Today, one of the aims of education is to bring about behavioural changes in the students in accordance with the objectives of the education or teaching. These are the standards that serve as measures of evaluation or achievement.

In mathematics also, evaluation occupies an important place. The achievement of the students and their interest and the aptitude with regard to mathematics can only be found out through the results of the examination. In fact, in the teaching of mathematics, it is more required.

In India, the entire system of education is examination geared. The main purpose of the teaching is to enable the students to pass the examination. It has a sense of respectability attached to it. If a particular person passes a particular examination, he is considered competent and a person who fails to do that is considered incompetent. The teaching of mathematics has, therefore, also to keep in view the importance of the examination.

Generally, the test or the methods of examinations are of two types. (1) Traditional or essay type examination, and (2) New type test or examination. Traditional type of test or traditional type of examination has only one form and that is essay type of examination. New types of examinations or tests are called objective type tests. They are of the following types.

1. Recall type of test.

   Ex: $a^m \div a^n =$ ———

2. Alternate response type of test.

   Ex: The sum of the two sides of a triangle is equal to the third side. Yes/No.

3. Multiple choice type of test.

   Ex: An obtuse angle can be equal to ( )
   (a) 90° (b) 75° (c) 60° (d) 120°

4. Matching type of test.

   Ex: Match the results with conditions

	Results		Conditions	
1.	75°	1.	Obtuse angle	( )
2.	360°	2.	Right angle	( )
3.	180°	3.	Acute angle	( )
4.	400°	4.	Angle at a point	( )
5.	90°	5.	Reflex angle	( )
6.	270°	6.	Straight angle	( )
7.	120°			

5. The completion type of test.

   Ex: The cube root of 125 is————

6. Classification type of test.

   Ex: Underline the word that does not belong to the group.

   Rectangle, Square, Triangle, Quadrilateral, Rhombus.

In fact, it is true and premature to think of giving up the essay type of test or the traditional type of test. What is needed is the removal of the defects of the traditional type of tests and the introduction of the new type of tests. This would make the examination system scientific. This is the truth with mathematics as well.

Background of the Study

Equalization of Educational Opportunities

Human society is not homogeneous. It is heterogeneous in nature. No two individuals are exactly alike. Human beings are differentiated from each other in physical appearance, intellectual capacity, perception ability, and moral, philosophical, religious and political aspects. The caste system,[30] the joint family system and the village system are often regarded as the three basic pillars of the Indian social system. The caste system is an inseparable component and a form of social stratification of Indian society. The caste system did not allow any freedom to individual to select his profession. Castes have elaborate restrictions on diet and on social mixing. The son of a carpenter could not become a weaver nor could a goldsmith become a tailor. This kind of rigid and stratified caste system gave them no opportunity to adopt themselves to the changing needs of the twentieth century.

The upper castes were the first to benefit by education during the British era. They held the highest government posts. At the bottom of the social ladder, the scheduled castes existed. Of these, the lowest and the most deprived were the untouchables who were prohibited many rights and highly isolated.

Mahatma Gandhi made a dramatic bid through his teaching and extensive tour of the country to wipe out the backwardness and the injustice to the untouchables. The Indian Constitution of 1950, through its Article 17, abolished untouchability and forbade its practice in any form. Act of Untouchability Offences that passed in 1955 provides penalties for discrimination in any form. There are also constitutional provisions for the socially and economically stratified classes for equality of educational opportunities and special reservation facilities for the socially and economically backward classes for entry into educational institutions and government jobs.

Article 46, a directive principle of the Indian constitution,[31] states that "The state shall promote with special care the educational and economic interests of the weaker sections of the people and in particular of the scheduled castes and the scheduled tribes..........".

Article 15, which proclaims the fundamental right of non-discrimination, has favoured (in claim 03) special treatment for women and children. And the very first amendment to the constitution, clause (4) to Article 15, specially mentions that the state may make "special provision for the advancement of any socially and educationally backward classes of the citizens or for the scheduled castes and scheduled tribes".

The Education Commission (1964-66) stressed the need for providing equality of educational opportunities to all sections of population belonging to different castes, regions and religions. Equalization of educational opportunity means providing suitable education for all in accordance with their interest, abilities and attitudes. The modern trend in the social change is towards the establishment of equality, freedom, justice and fraternity in the social order.

Origin of APSWR Schools

The terms 'Scheduled Caste' and 'Scheduled Tribe' are used mainly in the context of Indian society. The term 'Scheduled Caste' was first adopted in 1935 when the lowest ranking castes were listed in a schedule prepared by a commission appointed by the central government for the purpose of statutory safeguards and other benefits. This group is diverse and large. The members belong to numerous sub-castes, each of which has its own identity, traditions and characteristics. While the scheduled caste group was always a part of the regular society, the 'scheduled tribe' as the name suggests, refers to territorially bound communities. The bulk of them lives in the isolation of hills and forests. They have a distinct ethnic and cultural focus which gives them a separate identity.

The problems of the children from these communities are interwoven, each being a cause and effect of the other. For example, when the occupation of the family is menial, it does not fetch adequate wages, and low wages lead to poverty. This poverty often becomes the cause of ill-health, malnutrition, inferior surroundings or habitats. Parents of these children were also born in these conditions. They did not have access to schooling and education. The children of such houses try to earn their livings from a very young age. Naturally, they cannot go to school and hence they remain illiterate. Some children have to work for longer hours and they cannot go to schools. Many children live in villages and they do not have convenient schools.

In recent years, many measures have been initiated by the centre, the states and local bodies, at various levels to provide equality of opportunities to the weaker sections of the society. The children of scheduled castes and scheduled tribes have equal rights and opportunities with other children at school and this has been guaranteed by our constitutional provisions. Scholarships and stripends, free books, and tuition-free education are provided at school and also at college level. Adequate measures have been taken by the central and the state governments to provide proper facilities to the weaker sections of the nation, like the backward classes, the most backward classes, scheduled castes and scheduled tribes by way of offering free education, book grants, free lodging and boarding facilities and scholarships.

In accordance with the guidance given by the Constitution of India, the state government of Andhra Pradesh used residential school education as an innovative modern tool to provide standard education for socially and economically backward and weaker sections.

At present, in Andhra Pradesh, three types of residential schools are working to provide quality education for socially and economically backward pupils. They are

1. APSWR Schools
2. APTWR Schools
3. APR Schools

Andhra Pradesh Social Welfare Residential Schools (APSWR Schools) are working especially for scheduled caste (SC) children. In these schools, 75% of seats are allotted to SC category and 25% of seats are allotted to other backward classes. The schools are functioning under an autonomous body, APSWREI Society (Andhra Pradesh Social Welfare Residential Educational Institutions Society), with the budgets allotted by the Ministry of Social Welfare, Government of Andhra Pradesh.

Andhra Pradesh Tribal Welfare Residential Schools (APTWR Schools) are working especially for scheduled tribe (ST) children. In these schools, 75% of seats are allotted to ST category and 25% of seats are allotted to other backward classes. These schools are functioning under an autonomous body, APTWREI Society (Andhra Pradesh Tribal Welfare Residential Educational Institutions Society), with the budgets allotted by the Ministry of Tribal Welfare, Government of Andhra Pradesh.

Andhra Pradesh Residential Schools (APR Schools) are called general schools. In these schools 60% of seats are allotted to open category and 40% of seats are allotted to SC, ST and other backward classes. These schools are functioning under an autonomous body, APREI Society (Andhra Pradesh Residential Educational Institutions Society), with the budgets allotted by the Ministry of Education, Government of Andhra Pradesh.

The Government of Andhra Pradesh is making many changes to change its future and to make it glorious. Keeping this in mind, the APSWREI Society is moulding the career of SC students to provide a prominent place in future. The APSWR Schools are the progress steps for the children of scheduled castes.

'Gurukula System' in Residential Schools

Education has become indispensable for every one. The machinery of government is inadequate to educate all. According to earlier targets, we had to educate all children by the time they attain 14 years. The year 1960 was thought of as the year of fulfilling the target. Even though four decades have elapsed since then, we managed to educate about 62% of the total population.

On the old Indian educational scenario, the Gurukulas (residential places of learning) played a very prominent role in educating the pupils or disciples. Later on, this system failed to cope up with the changes that occurred in the society and disappeared almost, to say frankly, and a new set-up of educational institutions came into existence and took deep roots. With the new system introduced and implemented by the British, many people got educated and obtained proficiency and efficiency in many fields of education and vocation.

Though the formal system of educational set-up has been providing education at its best to its non-boarders, it has certain disadvantages which include poor teacher-taught relationship, improper discipline, poor achievement, irrelevant teaching and learning strategies, less teacher-pupil interaction and so on. At this time, the importance of residential system offered by the 'GURUKULAS' in good olden days was identified as the best system to solve many problems in educating a child and to provide quality education through better teaching-learning strategies. This thought gave rise to many residential schools and colleges. The central and state governments have established various residential educational institutions for different sectors of people and with suitable aims and objectives. In these institutions the teacher and the student live together in the same campus. This residential setup is providing hostel and educational facilities in a congenial atmosphere. Residential educational institutions are providing study in better living and educational conditions.

Why Selected this Topic for Study?

Every teacher has experienced the rise in pupil interest that comes with the introduction of a real problem situation one with which the pupils are genuinely concerned.[32] This phenomenon is especially noticeable if the problem has to do with the application of a mathematical principle that is being treated in the abstract.

Proper motivation of learning is one of the basic essentials of any set of educational experiences. The outcomes of such a vital experience are of different kinds, including certain knowledge, skills, abilities, understandings, attitudes, interests, appreciations and ways of living. Learning goes on the best in the degree that the individual sees and feels the significance to his own felt needs of what he does. Pupil's purpose is the prime move to the carrying out of learning experience.

The vital role of motivation in life and learning is indisputable.[33] Success and achievement in life and learning depend very largely on how much the student really want to succeed and achieve, what cost in human effort and energy the student is willing to bear to reach his goal, and what strong satisfactions he look forward to when he accomplishes his desire. In other words, the student's success and achievement in life and learning depends on his motivation. Motivation is the vital condition, the most powerful director of all learning. It is a factor in stimulating and directing learning. Teachers consider it as the art of stimulating and sustaining interest in learning.

Motivation is a process of including the activeness of an organism and determining its orientation.[34] Motivation is the force that energizes and gives direction to behaviour and that underlies the tendency to persist.[35] Etymologically, to motivate is to induce movement. Motives are conditions within the organism that induce it to act and behave in a certain way.[36]

Motives for learning are of several kinds. Purposes may be regarded as sources of intrinsic motivation, that is, they are inherent in the learning situation. Intrinsic motivation is found in the purposes, interests, needs, and attitudes of the learner. Extrinsic motivation resides in some condition outside of the learning situation. It's commonest forms are marks, prizes, rewards, etc., and scolding, sarcasm, threat and ridicule are its negative forms.

Motivation can be increased by increasing need-for-achievement. Motivation can be developed in stages in training programmes.[37] Training in behaviour such as how to take moderate risks, how to develop self-confidence in one's own ability to solve long range problems, how to be challenged by moderately difficult tasks, how to look for feed back of one's long range performance, and how to refer gratifications would help to develop a high need-for-achievement.

In 1938, Murray defined the need to achieve as a desire or tendency to overcome obstacles, to exercise power, to strive to do something difficult as well and as quickly as possible.[38]

McClelland's hypothesis is that the achievement motive is the mainspring of entrepreneurial activity fostering the economic development of a society.[39] McClelland found that too much pressure or too much perceived pressure may result in low achievement motivation. Other variables which are influential are sex of the child, size of the family, and occupation of father;

achievement motivation depends upon culture. He further observed that high achievers had developed an expectation of mastering challenging and difficult performances.

Achievement motive can be defined as the impetus to do well relative to some standard of excellence. A person with strong need achievement wants to be successful, at some challenging task, not for profit or status but merely for the sake of doing well.

Achievement motivation is the key factor in achieving success in any task we perform. Whatever one learns, motivation plays a dominant role in making to learn that thing. Motivation and learning are interdependent. If one wants to learn something, one should try to develop interest in that through motivation.

It is equally true for learning of mathematics. The proper foundation in the knowledge of the subject mathematics laid at school depends upon the motivation of the individual. Achievement motivation in learning mathematics may be aroused if we provide them opportunities of utilising their mental powers.

Mathematics is considered as a necessary subject for all the learners. It demands practice and application in the daily life which is possible only when the students have achievement motivation in learning. It is educationally unsound to teach mathematics if the students do not show any interest. So, the investigation intends to estimate achievement motivation of students.

If the students possess greater achievement motivation, they may be initiative, and confident to do the problems to be done in the class and from other books, and to satisfy their deep and extensive interest. They may go on to satisfying their intellectual hunger. It may be a leisure time activity also.

The achievements motivation may also influence their regularity, attention in the classes, their aspirations to achieve in terms of marks or solving the complex and challenging sums or puzzles, and their choice of friends based on their interest and so on. Achievement in mathematics depends on the learning of the student in the subject. It is seen from statistical analysis of the various examinations' results that achievement in mathematics is relatively low when compared with the other subjects.

Among the numerous reasons for pcor performance in mathematics, one of the reasons might be low motivation in the subject. Previous studies revealed that pupils having high motivation seem to achieve high scores in the subject. The level of achievement motivation of a student in the subject is responsible for the students achievement in that particular subject. Ahluwalia (1985) proved that academic performance was positively and significantly related with achievement motivation. Mansuri (1986)[40] found that the students having good general ability also had a high level of achievement motivation. Jayanthi (1989) proved that there is positive correlation between mathematical interest and academic achievement in mathematics.

As a teacher of mathematics, the investigator has personal interest in assessing and confirming the facts of the previous studies which established a relationship between achievement motivation and achievement taking the sample from APSWR Schools, as there are no studies relating to achievement motivation and achievement in mathematics with the present sample. Therefore, the investigator selected this topic and wanted to study the relationship between achievement motivation and academic achievement in mathematics.

The investigator felt that decisions can be clearly expressed by Xth class students than lower classes. So he had taken Xth class students as a sample for the study. Learning of such a vast, useful and accurate subject can't be possible if there is no motivation in the subject and also one can't cope up with the existing world without good knowledge in mathematics. Keeping all these in view, the investigator wanted to get solutions to the following questions.

1. What are the different levels of achievement motivation?
2. What are the different levels of achievement in Mathematics ?
3. Is there any difference in achievement motivation between boys and girls, rural and urban students. and SC and OBC students ?
4. Is there any difference in achievement in mathematics

between boys and girls, rural and urban students, and SC and OBC students?

5. What is the relationship between achievement motivation and achievement in mathematics ?

Documentation

1. Seetharamu, A.S., Philosophies of Education., 1989, p. 11.
2. Aggarwal, J.C., Theory and Principles of Education, 1995, p. 3.
3. Bhatia, K.K., Principles of Education, 1996, p. 8.
4. Aggarwal, op.cit., p. 5.
5. Charles, E. Skinner, Educational Psychology, 1984, pp. 26-28.
6. Shakuntala Devki, More Puzzles to Puzzle you, 1987, p. 2.
7. Papalia, D.E. and Sally Wendkos Olds, Psychology, 1987, p. 3.
8. Merlin, C. Wittrock, Hand book of Research on Teaching, 1986, p. 869.
9. Papalia and Sally, op.cit., p. 4.
10. Hans Raj Bhatia, A Textbook of Educational Psychology, 1965, p. 5.
11. Skinner, C.E., op.cit., p. 7. (Anderson, G.L., Educational Psychology and Teacher Education, Journal of Educational Psychology XL, (May 1949) pp. 275-284.)
12. Ibid., p. 7.
13. Bhatia, H.S., op.cit., pp. 9-14.
14. Sidhu, K.S., The Teaching of Mathematics, 1999, p. 169.
15. Mangal, S.K., Educational Psychology, 1998, p. 189.
16. Mangal, S.K., Advanced Educational Psychology, 1993, pp. 127-128.

17. Husen. T. and Postlethwaite, T. N., The International Encyclopedia of Education, 1985, p. 3427.

18. Morris, L.B. and Maurice P.H., Psychological Foundations of Education, 1980, p.96.

19. Mangal, S.K., Advanced Educational Psychology, op.cit., pp. 119-120.

20. Ibid., p. 129. (McClelland, D.C., Atkinson J.W. Clark and Lowell, E.C., The Achievement Motive, 1953)

21. Mangal, Educational Psychology, op.cit., p.198.

22. Mangal, Advanced Educational Psychology, op.cit., p. 129 (Atkinson, J.W and Feather, N.T., A Theory of Achievement Motivation, 1966, p.13).

23. Chauhan, S.S., Advanced Educational Psychology, 1978, pp. 203-204.

24. Morris and Maurice, op.cit., p. 101.

25. Herbet, J.W. and Geneva, D.H., International Encyclopedia of Educational Evaluation, 1990, pp. 3-9.

26. Hans Raj Bhatia, op.cit., p. 526.

27. Sidhu, K.S., op.cit., p. 201.

28. Skinner, C.E., op.cit., p. 677.

29. Rai, B.C., Method of Teaching of Mathematics, 1981, p. 81.

30. Philosophy of Education (M.Ed., Study Material), Bharati Dasan University, 1997, pp. 236-241.

31. Kamat, A.R., Educational and Social change in India, 1985, p. 247.

32. Aggarwal, S.M., A Course of Teaching of Modern Mathematics, 1987, p. 104.

33. Hans Raj Bhatia, op.cit., pp. 257-260.

34. Petrovsky, A.V. and Yaroshevsky, M.G., A Concise Psychology Dictionary, 1985, p. 193.

35. Papalia and Sally, op.cit, p. 344.
36. Hans Raj Bhatia, op.cit., p. 258.
37. Pillai, J.K., Effective Teaching, 1999, p. 100.
38. Papalia and Sally, op.cit., p. 334.
39. Pillai, op.cit., p. 99.
40. Buch, M.B., Fourth Survey of Research in Education, 1991, pp.333.

2

Review of Related Studies

Overview

This chapter attempts to survey and critically review studies related to the theme of the investigator chosen for his study. It consists of six sections. This one is an overview of the entire chapter. The second section briefly brings out the rationale of the survey and review. The third one outlines briefly a number of Indian studies related to the investigation. The fourth section outlines briefly of foreign studies related to the investigation. The fifth section is a critical review of the studies cited. The final section furnishes the documentary notes for the references made in the chapter.

The 'Why' of the Review

A summary of the writings of recognized authorities and of previous research provides evidence that the researcher is familiar with what is already known and what is still unknown and untested[1]. Since effective research is based upon past knowledge, this step helps to eliminate the duplication of what has been done and provides useful hypotheses and helpful suggestions for significant investigation.

A knowledge of related literature enables the investigator to define the frontiers of his field : an understanding of the different theories in the field will enable him to place his question in proper perspective; one learns about the procedures and instruments that have proved useful and also those which seem less promising; a thorough search through related research avoids unintentional replication of previous studies; it places the researcher in a better position to interpret the significance of his own results[2].

In searching related literature the researcher should note certain important elements[3].

(a) Reports of closely related studies that have been investigated.

(b) Design of the study, including procedures employed and data-gathering instruments used.

(c) Populations that were sampled : sampling methods employed.

(d) Variables that were defined.

(e) Extraneous variables that could have affected the findings.

(f) Faults that could have been avoided.

(g) Recommendations for further research.

The search for related literature is a time consuming process, even though it is necessary, as earlier stated, for a good research work. Hence, this chapter, Review of Related Studies, is meant for the study of objectives that lead to the inclusion of achievement motivation in the school programmes and the level of achievement required in mathematics to students of various courses. It is also meant for the study of the research works related to achievement motivation, achievement in mathematics and the inter-relationship between these two factors of mathematics education.

The National Policy on Education (1986)[4] also highlights the important role of Mathematics as, "Mathematics should be visualized as the vehicle to train a child to think, reason, analyze and to articulate logically. Apart from being a specific subject, it should be treated as a concomitant to any subject involving analysis and reasoning."

Mathematics is one of the compulsory subjects of secondary education. The main aim of teaching mathematics at the secondary school level is to train the mind, develop the power of understanding and critical thinking among the pupils. The richness and the utility of mathematics lie in problems of mathematics and hence, the learning of mathematics becomes congruent with the ability of solving mathematical problems.

Mathematics contributes to effective citizenship. Mathematics as an expression of human mind reflects the active will, the contemplative reason, and the desire for aesthetic perfection. Its basic elements are logic and intuition, analysis and construction, generality and individuality.

Mathematics is a way to settle in the mind, a habit of reasoning. Mathematics is essentially a programme of education, which fosters higher order mental processes such as questioning, reasoning, analyzing, inducing and logical thinking. Hence, the teaching of mathematics attains utmost importance in any school curriculum.

Mathematics exhibits fully the power of man to think consistently and logically[5]. It satisfies the thirst for knowledge, the love of truth and beauty and the desire to interpret and control environment. Motivation should be provided through intellectual curiosity and through applications to other fields of study. It may also be provided through the application of mathematics to business, industry and the professional fields. Motivation may be provided through emphasis on cultural, social and educational values.

Motives for learning are of several kinds. Purposes may be regarded as sources of intrinsic motivation, i.e., they are inherent in the learning situation. Intrinsic motivation is found in the purposes, interests, needs, and attitudes of the learner. Extrinsic motivation resides in some condition outside of the learning situation. Its commonest forms are marks, prizes, rewards, etc., and scolding, sarcasm, threats and ridicule are its negative forms.

Motivation arouses interest in the learning. It is the central factor in effective management of the process of learning. If a student is motivated properly he will have adequate achievement motivation. Achievement motivation may be associated with a variety of goals. In general, the behaviour adopted will involve an activity which is directed towards the attainment of some standard of excellence.

Indian Studies

Achievement Motivation

In this section an attempt is made to present an account of salient studies done on Indian samples, with special references to factors associated with growth of achievement motive and its behavioural correlates.

Mishra (1967)[6] studied certain personality correlates of need achievement among university students. The study reveals that a high n-ach person tends to be less authoritarian, reacts to frustration, is less anxious and had high level of adjustment.

Abrol (1977) studied achievement motivation in relation to intelligence, vocational interests, achievement, sex and SES (Socio-Economic Status). Boys tend to have higher achievement motivation than girls. SES and family affect achievement motivation. Gupta (1979) reported a positive relationship between psychological stress and achievement motivation. Zargar (1980) studied need achievement in relation to intelligence, creativity, and scholastic achievement. Need achievement has a positive relationship with non-verbal creativity.

Rajeeva (1982) studied achievement motive, its correlates and performance. Dhillon (1979) studied achievement motivation pattern of students who participate in physical activities and of those who do not participate. Narula (1979) studied achievement motivation in relation to intelligence, SES and performance of prospective secondary school teachers in Orissa. Intelligence, it reports, is independent of n-ach.

Previous reviews by Rao, Mehta and Rao (1979)[7] indicate a growing interest in achievement motivation research covering the period 1967-75. The research has primarily concentrated on the antecedents of n-ach, n-ach and achievement relationships, developments of n-ach measures and motivation training. The intervention studies to enhance n-ach among school children are a remarkable feature of research on the Indian scene[8].

Jain (1983)[9] in his study found that intelligence was found to be a better predictor of concept formation ability than achievement motivation. There exists no significant sex difference in the concept formation ability of four extreme groups, namely high intelligence - high achievement motivation group, high intelligence - low achievement motivation group, low intelligence - high achievement motivation group and low intelligence - low achievement motivation group. Verbal intelligence was found to have the greatest significant interactional effect on concept formation, where as achievement motivation was placed at the second position in this respect. There existed positive linear significant relationship between the student's scores on concept formation and achievement motivation.

Sinha (1986)[10] in his doctoral study found that prejudices influenced achievement motivation in a negative way and high prejudiced males and females had higher achievement motivation.

According Raghava (1985)[11], the achievement motivation development (AMD) training resulted in the increase in independence in pupils and the AMD course improved the n-ach of the pupils. Academic motivation did not influence the gain scores in n-ach, performance adjustment, dependency, classroom trust and performance. No sex differences were seen in n-ach.

Ahluwalia (1985)[12] stated that : Sex of the child had no effect on achievement motivation, Age was significantly and positively related to achievement motivation, Achievement motivation was not affected by birth order, Academic performance was positively and significantly related with achievement motivation, Father's education significantly affected achievement motivation while mother's education had no effect on achievement motivation of children, The achievement motivation was not affected either by father's occupation or mother's occupation, Economic status of parents did not affect achievement motivation, Urban/rural up bringing of children had no effect on achievement motivation of children, Size of family did not show any significant relationship with achievement motivation, Dependency and achievement motivation were found to be negatively related though not significantly, Children of co-educational schools had more achievement motivation than children of boys schools. But no significant influence was recorded in the children of co-educational schools and girls schools, those of boys schools and girls schools, Children from central schools were most achievement motivated and next in order were public and then government schools, The organizational climate in different types of schools did not significantly affect the achievement motivation of children.

Abrol (1977) found that achievement motivation scores did not differ in the case of boys or girls. Achievement motivation was higher among those students who have more of vocational interest maturity. Achievement motivation and scholastic achievement were correlated positively.[13]

Gupta (1978) stated that the low anxiety group had higher mean achievement motivation than the high anxiety group, but the differences were not statistically significant. Boys were more achievement motivated than girls. In the case of boys there was negative relationship between anxiety and achievement motivation. In the case of groups belonging to low economic status and having middle academic achievement, correlation between anxiety and achievement motivation was positive.[14]

Rajeeva (1982) found a significant difference between classroom trust scores of high and low achievement motivation students. There was significant difference between the achievement scores of high achievement motivation students.[15]

Zargar (1980) found no significant relationship between the level of expression and the scholastic achievement. The high need achievers had a better scholastic achievement than the low need achievers.[16]

Bharathi (1984)[17] in her study obtained the result that the strength of achievement motivation increased significantly from twelve years to sixteen years. At different age levels different self-concept measures were found to be related with n-achievement. No sex differences were found in achievement motivation.

Achievement motivation was found to be the highest among the high SES (Socio-Economic Status) groups and lowest in low SES groups.

Mansuri (1986)[18] in his study with the students of V, VI and VII found that grade was an effective variable in achievement motivation. The differences among means of grades V, VI and VII were significant and in favour of successive grades. The students of successive grades showed successive advancement in achievement motivation. The students having high-level motivation towards school were better in achievement motivation than those with a low level of motivation toward school. The interaction effect between grade and motivation towards school was not significant. The students having good general ability also had a high level of achievement motivation. The interaction effect between grade and general ability was not significant.

Singh (1986)[19] found that correlations between n-ach and (a) intellectual efficiency, (b) introversion-extroversion, (c) socio-cultural status and (d) mathematics achievement were found significant. The difference in mathematics achievement was significant for low and high groups in n-ach in case of Delhi schools but in case of Haryana schools it was not significant. The difference in mathematics achievement among boys, identified as belonging to the same socio-cultural status of Delhi and Haryana schools after having the effect of achievement motivation and intellectual efficiency controlled statistically was significant.

Tiwari (1984)[20] found that privileged students scored significantly higher in achievement motivation than deprived ones. Privileged pupils, boys and girls, scored significantly higher than the deprived boys and girls, on factors of F and J of HSPQ (High School Personality Questionnaire) whereas with respect to factor H, I, Q, deprived pupils, boys and girls outscored the privileged ones.

Chattargi (1983)[21], based on his study, stated that scores of achievement motivation of students of science and commerce were significantly higher than those of other groups.

Chauhan (1984)[22] found that the students of scheduled caste and scheduled tribe did not differ significantly in relation to their achievement motivation. Scheduled caste boys and girls had slightly higher achievement motivation than the scheduled tribe boys and girls. The achievement motivation of students differed significantly at different levels of socio-economic status - high, middle and low. Community, sex and socio-economic status did not interact significantly in relation to the achievement motivation of students.

Khanna (1982)[23] found that the n-ach was significant on all achievement related words. The main effect of n-ach was significant on achievement related statements.

Lalitha (1982)[24] found that there was no significant difference in mean scores of tribal and non-tribal students in achievement motivation. There were no sex differences in the mean n-achievement scores of boys and girls within tribal and non-tribal samples. The residential tribal school children had demonstrated better school achievement than the tribal and non-tribal children in common schools.

Gokulnathan (1971) and Gokulnathan and Mehta (1972)[25] have reported higher need for achievement in tribal students than non-tribal students and in girls than boys. One would have expected a lower level of need for achievement in tribal boys as they belong to the socially disadvantaged group. Perhaps the explanation is in the special nature of the sample. The tribal boys who had migrated from a village to some urban areas and were studying in some urban based school, showed significantly greater need for achievement than their non-tribal counterparts (Gokulnathan and Mehta, 1972). A similar trend favouring tribal boys was found in a subsequent NCERT study (NCERT, 1970). Mehta (1968) has reported a curvilinear relationship between need for achievement and fathers' education. Significant differences were found in groups with high and low fathers' education.

Achievement in Mathematics

Achievement in mathematics has been studied in relation to a number of variables, both cognitive and affective.[26] Studies have confirmed that intelligence and socio-economic background are major contributions to mathematics achievement (Singh 1986; Nilima Kumari, 1984; Rajput, 1984; Gakhar, 1981; Jabbal, 1981; Kabu, 1980; Nalinidevi, 1986). Factors responsible for poor achievement or failure have also caught the attention of researchers. Mainka (1983) found language mastery was an important factor in the acquisition of concepts in mathematics.

Nilima Kumari (1984) studied the conservation of number and substance in relation to intelligence and SES, revealing significant positive relationships. Reasoning power, space visualizations, attitude towards mathematics were found significantly related to mathematics achievement (Patel, 1984).

In Rajput's (1984) study, achievement motivation was found to have no bearing upon achievement. Gakhar (1981) identified variables of educational environment as responsible for acquisition of mathematical concepts. Apart from SES and intelligence, variables like teacher's qualifications, class size, encouragement to teacher by the head, use of audio-visual aids, and feed back were found significantly related to acquisition of mathematical concepts.

Katiyar's (1979) study revealed that boys and girls did not differ in mathematics achievement. Singh (1986) found attitudes to be related to mathematics achievement. Factors predominant among failures were mathematical background, attitude towards mathematics and low motivation (Jain, 1979).

Gadgil (1979) also studied the causes of failures at the SSC examination and found that school factors like inadequate coverage of the syllabus, inadequate attention to difficult topics and personal factors, like lack of motivation had been responsible for failures. Factors responsible for underachievement in mathematics have been some personality variables, namely, self reliance, sense of personal freedom, feeling of belongingness, withdrawing tendencies, nervous symptoms, social skills, general anxiety and test anxiety, parental profession and parental education (Iyer, 1977). Tuli (1979) found that aptitude for mathematics was significantly and positively related to mathematical creativity.

Sarala (1990)[27] analysed the conceptual errors of secondary schools students in learning in selected areas of modern mathematics and found that the number of errors were quite large and these errors were influenced by sex, locality of the school, management of the school, intelligence, study habits and socio-economic status.

Khatoon (1988)[28] studied the relationship of mathematical aptitude of boys and girls with interest and vocational preferences. Though Khatoon did find no significant difference in the aptitude for mathematics among boys and girls, he found a significant difference in achievement.

Rasaly (1982) found that the attitude of high school students towards the learning of mathematics and their achievement in mathematics were highly correlated and that urban boys and girls had a more positive attitude towards mathematics than rural boys and girls.

Hariharan (1992) found that girls, urban students and private school students had more positive attitude towards homework in mathematics than others and that students with this positive attitude towards homework had better academic achievements in mathematics.

Chitkara (1985)[29] found that boys and girls of superior ability did not show any significant difference between their mean scores on achievement in mathematics. Girls of average ability scored significantly higher in mathematics than boys of average ability.

Bhaskara Rao and Pushpalatha (1996) found that the secondary school students were holding high achievement in mathematics. And also they found that the rural and urban students were possessing average achievement in mathematics with significant difference between them.

Vyas (1983)[30] in his research found that the students of the experimental group who were given a treatment of the SPLP (Symbol Picture Logic Programme) showed better achievement in mathematics than the control group students. The achievement in mathematics was independent of these three variables, namely, the programme, intelligence and syllogistic reasoning ability when there was no interaction among the three variables.

John Babu (2001)[31] found that the achievement of students preferring scientific, mechanical and socio-economic problem situations is significantly better than the achievement of students preferring the abstract problem situations.

Sridevi (1994)[32] found in her study that the achievement in mathematics of Intermediate students was high. The achievement in residential and non-residential colleges was different. Boys and girls differed in achievement in mathematics and boys scored high and the girls secured an average achievement.

Soujanya Mary (2000)[33] found in her study that most of the students were having high interest in Mathematics. The positive influence of family members, career prospects and achievement possibly might have made the students to be interested in mathematics.

Rathaiah and Bhaskara Rao (1998) found that the achievement of urban students was significantly better than the rural students.

Achievement Motivation and Achievement in Mathematics

Studies which have investigated achievement motivation as a factor in relation to academic achievement, in general, caution researchers to be careful while drawing inferences.[34]

Studies by Shanmugasundaram (1983), Deshpande (1984) and Sween (1984) indicated a positive relation between the two variables. But Rajput (1984) and Sontakey (1986) did not indicate any such relation. Mitra (1985) throws a better light on the issue. The study found that the achievement motivation was positively and significantly correlated with academic achievement, but this result was not arrived at when intelligence is partialled out.

According to Sharma (1981), poor academic motivation, poor linguistic ability, poor planning of study work, poor adjustment and emotional insecurity contributed to under-achievement of rural girls in secondary schools of Haryana.

Mehta (1987)[35] found that the students who had high achievement motivation achieved higher school achievement when one of the independent variables was attitude towards parents and teachers. Similarly, the students having high achievement motivation achieved high in school achievement and when one of the independent variables was attitude towards discipline. Not a single interaction was significant when one of the independent variables was attitude towards parents and teachers. Four interactions were significant when one of the independent variables was attitude towards discipline. When the variables achievement motivation, caste, adjustment and, achievement motivation and caste were joined with the variable attitude towards discipline, they influenced the school achievement of the pupils.

Rajput (1984)[36] in his study obtained the results that in neutral classroom conditions, the achievement of students in mathematics was not affected by their achievement motivation. The socio-economic status of the children affected the achievement of students in mathematics. The double and triple interaction effects between the variables of intelligence achievement motivation and socio-economic status were not significant.

Aruna (1981) stated that the academic achievement of SC and ST students studying in standard VII was significantly lower than that of general population. The academic achievement of ST students was superior to that of SC students. The academic achievement of SC and ST students studying in rural schools was inferior to that of their counterparts in urban schools. The academic achievement of boys (SCs and STs taken together) was superior to that of girls. There was a significant correlation of 0.44 between the intelligence and the academic achievement of SC and ST students.[37]

Gandhi (1982) stated that there was no significant sex difference with respect to achievement motive. High school girls had significantly higher motive to affiliate than high schools boys. Achievement motive was significantly and positively related to academic achievement of high school students of both the sexes. The academic achievement of high school boys and girls was significantly affected by their scores on high, average and low levels of affiliation motive. Affiliation motive significantly affected the academic achievement of high school boys; however, it did not affect high school girls' academic achievement. High, average and low levels of power motive did not affect the academic achievement of either high school boys or girls significantly.[38]

Rani (1980) found that the SC students' academic achievement was significantly lower than that of the non-SC students. Both differed significantly with regard to physical self-concept, self-esteem and self-concept. There was no difference in the SC and the non-SC students with respect to the achievement anxiety and perception of purpose in life. The academic achievement of the students was positively related to reflected self-esteem of two other significant factors (teachers and peers) in the educational set-up for the SC students. No significant relationship existed between academic achievement and achievement anxiety and perception of purpose in life for both SC and non-SC students.[39]

Singh and Rajeshwar Prasad (1983)[40] conducted a study on the under and over academic achievement and its motivational correlates. They derived two factors from correlation matrix of under achievement at 'I' level. One factor was named the 'motivation factor'. The second factor operative in this group was labelled as the 'self debasing factor'. The motivational organization of under achievers was found to be significantly less harmonious than that of over achievers.

Singh (1984) found that self-concept of academic ability was significantly and positively related to academic motivation. Sex differences were unrelated to self-concept of academic ability and need for achievement motivation.

Vimla (1985)[41] found that there was a highly significant and positive relationship between achievement motivation scores of track athletes and their performance scores. There was significant difference in performance in track events between athletes having high and low achievement motivation. The high achievement motivation athletes had high performance in track events.

Dutt (1983)[42] found that the tribal students with high achievement motivation were better than students having low achievement motivation with regard to intelligence and extroversion. There was no effect of achievement motivation of tribal students on their anxiety, emotional adjustment, social adjustment, educational adjustment, neuroticism and perception, parental support, parental control and parental punishment.

Fatmi (1986) found that the racial background, sex, religious background and caste status influenced achievement related motivations. Non-tribals, girls, caste, Hindus and forward and backward caste groups were superior in achievement-related motivations. The achievement motivation of a person had a significantly positive correlation with other achievement-related motivations.

Foreign Studies

Ever since McClelland (1953) turned from the laboratory to the analysis of economic development and the role of achievement motivation in stimulating societal growth, the achievement motive has aroused wide spread interest among psychologists leading to a plethora of studies all over the world. A number of psychologists have come to the conclusion that in Indian society especially in its rural segment achievement motive is low. Naturally, it is assumed that the socio-cultural-ethos of the rural society must not be congenial for healthy growth of achievement motive.

Achievement motivation is the desire to do better to achieve unique accomplishment, to compete with a standard of excellence, and to involve one self with long term achievement goals. The theory of achievement motivation has been developed by David C. McClleland at the Harvard University and John W. Atkinson at the University of Michigan.

Studies on achievement motivation were begun by a group of American researches headed by David McClelland. They proposed the theory and methodology of measuring achievement motivation which were further elaborated in the works of John Atkinson and Heinz Heckhansen.[43]

It is an established fact that human behaviour reflects variability, purpose, and order.[44] The concept of motivation has been propounded by psychologists to explain the dynamics of these behavioural properties. The current conception of human motivation derives its origin from the classic work of Murray (1938). He advanced the view that personality is a configuration of some basic psychogenic needs or motives. A need, according to Murray, is basically a lack of something vital to the organism, such as water, nourishment and oxygen. The socio-psycological needs are extensions of this basic idea. Murray has also developed a projective measure of these needs widely known as TAT (Thematic Apperception Test). McClelland opened a new vista in motivational psychology through his experimental studies aimed at discovering whether or not, and, if so, how motivation was expressed in the content of imaginary stories. The earlier studies conducted by McClelland and Atkinson (1948) and by Atkinson and McClelland (1948) revealed that TAT was undoubtedly sensitive to motivational influences. Realizing the significance of this finding, McClelland and his associates (1949) initiated a research programme to study achievement motive, a particular aspect of human motivation, in great detail.

Achievement motive has been conceptualized as an individual's orientation to endeavour for conduction of activities in those situations where the performance has to be evaluated. As a motive force, it functions in the form of a relative stable characteristic of personality, after the period of early socialization during which it develops (Atkinson, 1958).

According to McClelland and others, achievement motivation is formed during the child's up bringing in the family, under the influence of his parents, firstly of his mother. A special projective method was worked out for the qualitative estimation and study of achievement motivation. An ambiguous picture was presented to the subject and he was asked to write what was happening, what is being thought of, what has led to this situation and what will happen. Pictures suggested a work situation (two men working at a machine), a study situation (a boy seated at a desk with a book in front of him), and a father-son situation (McClelland 1953).[45]

In 1938, Murray defined that the need to achieve as a desire or tendency "to overcome obstacles, to exercise power, to strive to do something difficult as well and as quickly as possible".[46]

It wasn't until 1953, however, that psychologists tried to measure the strength of this need using the Thematic Apperception Test (TAT) to do so (McClelland, Atkinson, Clark and Lowell, 1953).

We know that even 2 month-old babies seem to experience some sense of achievement since an experiment in which infants controlled the movement of an overhead mobile by turning, their heads found that the babies who did this seemed to smile more when the mobile moved than did babies who saw the same kind of mobile but hadn't made it move themselves (Watson and Ramey, 1972).

Several personality characteristics and behavioural styles of high achievement need people have also emerged. When given a choice of hard, easy, and in-between tasks they usually pick the in-between, which seems to present enough of a challenge to be interesting but not so much to be discouraging (Mahone, 1960; Morris, 1966). They are usually optimistic about their chances of success, consider themselves capable of it, take personal responsibility for it, and are willing to delay gratification to achieve it (Feather, 1965; Kukla, 1972; Mischel, 1961).

It is possible that the need for achievement may be atleast partly inherited; some people may be born with the drive to succeed. There are ways to increase need to achieve, that certain styles of child rearing seem to influence children to become high achievers (Feshbach and Weiner, 1982).

In one classic study, Winter bottom (1958) found that mothers of children with strong achievement motivation tend to encourage independence and mastery before their children are 8 years old, expecting their youngsters to know their way around the city and to do well in competition.

Achievement performance can also be improved later in life. Men who took part in a three-to-six week training course achieved more afterward than men who had not taken the course (McClelland and Winterbottom, 1969).

Since achievement motive is a learned disposition, the manner through which, the extent to which, it is learned, is largely determined by the society in which one grows up. Therefore, the attempts at studying the factors governing origin and growth of n-ach have been focussed at identifying environment orientation.[47]

McClelland (1951) has argued that psychogenic motives are learnt through association of primary biological pleasure and pain. According to him, all motives are learned. They develop out of repeated affective experiences connected with certain types of situations and certain types of behaviours (McClelland, *et.z al.* 1953). He considers early childhood as the ideal time to form strong affective associations which are so general that they will be hard to distinguish. In his analysis, McClelland found that there are four basic conditions which determine the strength of affective associations. They are privacy, involvement of the autonomic nervous system, time discrimination and intensity, and frequency of reward.

McClelland (1961) has made a large scale study of the growth pattern of achievement motive across a large number of countries and cultures. He has tried to determine the conditions which cause n-ach levels to change. He has distinguished between factors essential to development of n-ach. He has concluded that race and environment, as such, are not essential factors for growth of achievement motive. However, degree of environmental challenge can be considered as an essential factor. Dealing with child rearing practices, he says that early training of children to be independent and to master certain skills, promotes high n-ach, if that training does not indicate rejection of the child by the parents.

In an attempt to delineate the origin of n-ach, McClelland and Friedman (1952) observed that the degree of independence training is positively related to achievement imagery in folk literature. The number of experiences in mastery are characterized as an important antecedent of n-ach. Winterbottom (1958) has found that early parental demands for mastery and independence are positively related to development of high n-ach. Rosen and D'Andrade (1959) have reported that it was achievement training which determined growth of n-ach. Cross-cultural results reported by Child, Storm and Veroff (1965) and Moss and Kagan (1963) also share similar trends.

College men who were high in n-ach in their early twenties tended to end up in entrepreneurial jobs (McClelland, 1965).

In studies of men in fifteen fields of creative endeavour and in ten fields of governmental, judicial and military leadership, a strong relationship has shown up between achievement motivation and career success (Veroff, Atkinsen, Feld and Gurin, 1960).

The need to achieve is modified in some people by their need to avoid failure (Atkinson, 1957). Those with a high need to avoid failure are relevant to take the risks required to succeed.

Horner (1968) suggested that women have a "fear of success" that keeps them away from achieving. Subsequent researchers have come to different conclusions, including the fact that males experience, just as much fear of success as women (Tresemer, 1974). Today, then, many psychologists treat Horner's findings with some skepticism (Zuckerman and Wheeler 1975).

Nevertheless, several studies have confirmed the basic premise that women were having trouble reconciling their new-found freedom to achieve with traditional expectations about the role of women in society (Stephan, Rosenfield and Stephen, 1976; Kruegar, 1983).

Some women do feel ambivalent about achievement and may not compete because of what they see as the costs of achievement. There is considerable evidence that women often don't compete against men when they think a task involves "masculine" skills (Deaun, White and Farris, 1975).

McCelland (1961) has proposed that the relationship between the age at which parental demands are made and the strength of n-ach is curvilinear. Bartlett and Smith (1968) found that mothers of high n-ach boys make fewer demands for achievement and independence. The age at which demands are made was not related to the strength of n-ach. Pattern of reward training has also been observed to be related to n-ach (Davids and Hainsworth, 1967; Epps, 1970).

In a number of studies, evidence has been accumulated from different cultures and countries, i.e., U. S. A. (Rosen, 1962), India (Srivastava and Tiwari, 1967), Brazil (Angeline, et. al.,) coming from low socio-economic stratum of society show low level of n-ach. On the other hand, some studies (e.g. Uhr et. al., 1969 : Nygard, 1969) have demonstrated an increase in n-ach score as the socio-economic status increases. Soares and Soares (1971) have found that disadvantaged children have greater discrepancy between aspiration and achievement. The absence of one or both parents has been found to be significantly associated with low achievement tendency (Santrock and Wholford, 1970). Lott and Lott (1963) have reported that Whites have reliably stronger in n-ach than the Negroes. They have explained this discrepancy on the basis of background factors, i.e., socio-economic and cultural factors.[48]

Crandall, Katkovsky and Preston (1960) have vaguely assumed that n-ach develops somehow from ontogenetically earlier motives leaving in the dark the nature of these early motives. Martian Winterbottom's comparison between mothers of 8 to 10 years old boys of high and low n-ach has been a very stimulating study (Winterbottom, 1958). In this study mothers of high n-ach children were found to expect earlier independence (especially in decision-making) and mastery than the mothers of the low n-ach subjects. Several other independent studies have also confirmed the importance of early independence training (e.g., Heckhausen and Kemmler, 1957), and early maternal acceleration for manifested achievement behaviour in later life periods (Feld, 1967). A follow-up of some of Winterbottom's subjects showed high adolescent test-anxiety when mother had not encouraged independence in early childhood.

However, Hayashi and Yamaushi (1964) failed to corroborate Winterbottom's results in Japan. They found a reverse relationship. Japanese mothers expected self-reliance from their children much earlier than American and German mothers. It may be that Japanese mothers demand too much of their children too early. Regarded this way, it is no longer a paradox that very early independence training results in low achievement motivation. Veroff (1965) has presented theoretical considerations about the consequences of parental demands that miss the optimal development stage by coming either too early or too late.

Recent research focussing on n-ach has shifted away from concern with child rearing antecedents to situational determinants. How the person defines a situation affects the expression of n-ach in behaviour. Important in this definition are the values and goals that the person perceives in the situation. For example, Kahl (1965) found that the relation between n-ach and grades in college holds only for those students who perceive that grades are instrumental for future career success (Raynor, 1970).

Features of the situation that affect a person's attribution of success or failure to his own efforts and abilities rather than to chance or luck also appear to be crucial in determining whether predictions from the theory will be borne out (Fearther, 1967). The differentials in perception and their effects have been studied by Coleman, et. al. (1966); Weiner and Kukla (1970) and found that the causation of events and their reinforcing consequences may be viewed as either internal (under their own control) or external (beyond their own control). Rotter (1966) has noted a number of ways in which views of success and failure affect behaviour. Since strongly motivated individuals generally ascribe success to their efforts, they experience more reward, and thus, are more active in attempting to achieve. They also persist longer because they are more likely to ascribe failure to the lack of efforts than to a lack of ability. Finally, they prefer tasks of intermediate difficulty, since these yield most information about their own capabilities (Weiner and Kukla, 1970).

McClelland (1961) found that young entrepreneurs had higher n-ach than the old ones. Rosen (1959) has noted that subjects having low education had lowest n-ach and subjects with middle class education had highest n-ach. The subjects with highest education had somewhat less n-ach on the average than subjects with middle class education.

Several studies have shown that the socio-economic status is an important determinant of motivational level (Rosen, 1959; Leshan, 1952; Mischel, 1960; Douvan, 1956; McClelland, 1961; Fraser, 1961). In general, middle class children are found significantly higher in n-ach than lower class children.

Summary of the Related Studies

The need to achieve is the spring board of the achievement motive. Development of achievement motive is affected by a number of variables in home, school and society.

According McClelland and his associates, human beings differ from one another in the strength of achievement motive. This difference in the strength of motivation to achieve is important in understanding the differences in the economic growth of nations.

Tiwari, Bharathi and Chatterji found a high achievement motivation in their studies.

Ahluwalia found that the organizational climate in different types of schools did not affect the achievement motivation of children.

Bharathi, Sinha, Gandhi, Raghava, Lalitha, Jain and Ahluwalia found that the boys and girls were possessing achievement motivation without any significant difference between them. Abrol and Gupta found that the boys tend to have higher achievement motivation than girls.

Ahluwalia found that the rural and urban students were holding an average achievement motivation without any significant difference between them.

Soares and Soares, and Ahluwalia found that the disadvantaged children have greater discrepancy between aspiration and achievement.

Sridevi and Bhaskara Rao found that the students were holding high achievement in mathematics.

Gadgil found that school factors like inadequate coverage of syllabus, inadequate attention to difficult topics and personal factors, lack of motivation had been responsible for failures.

The studies of Katiyar, Khatoon, Chitkara found that the boys and girls were holding high achievement in mathematics. Katiyar's study revealed that the boys and girls did not differ in the achievement in mathematics.

Rosaly, Bhaskara Rao and Pushpalatha, and Rathaiah and Bhaskara Rao found that the urban students were possessing high achievement than rural students.

Rani found that the SC students' academic achievement was significantly lower than that of the non-SC students. Chauhan also found that SC boys and girls had slightly high achievement motivation than ST boys and girls.

Singh, Mehta, Rajput, Vimala and Fatima found a significant association between achievement motivation and academic achievement. Rajput found that the achievement of students in mathematics was not affected by their achievement motivation. Ahluwalia and Abrol found that the academic performance was positively and significantly related with achievement motivation.

Gandhi and Aruna found that the academic achievement of boys was superior to that of girls and achievement motive was significantly and positively related to the academic achievement of high school students of both sexes.

This summary reveals that there were no studies on achievement motivation and achievement in mathematics of the students exclusively studying in social welfare residential schools run only by the government(s). So, a study has been undertaken to study the level of achievement motivation and achievement in mathematics possessed by the students of social welfare residential schools and the association between the achievement motivation and achievement in mathematics.

Documentation

1. John W. Best, Research in Education , 1982, p. 40.

2. Donald Ary, Lucy Cheser Jacobs and Asghar Razavich, Introduction to Research in Education, 1972, p. 56.

3. Best, op.cit., p. 41.

4. John Babu, CH, Rajendra Prasad, T.J., Madhukar, G.M. and Bhaskara Rao, D., Problem Solving in Mathematics, 2001, p. 4.

5. Aggarwal, S.M., A Course in Teaching of Modern Mathematics, 1987, pp. 392-393.

6. Buch, M.B., Third Survey in Research in Education, 1987, p. 310

7. Buch, op.cit., p. 310.

8. Buch, M.B., Fourth Survey in Research in Education, 1991, p. 372.

9. Ibid., p. 374.

10. Ibid., p. 444.

11. Ibid., p. 421.

12. Ibid., p. 333.

13. Buch, Third Survey, op.cit., p. 317.

14. Ibid., p. 357.

15. Ibid., p. 399.

16. Ibid., p. 439.

17. Buch, Fourth Survey, op.cit., p. 340.

18. Ibid., p. 398.

19. Ibid., p. 436.

20. Ibid., p. 450.

21. Ibid., p. 351.

22. Ibid., p. 354.

23. Ibid., p. 383.

24. Ibid., p. 393.

25. Tiwari, A.N., Achievement Motivation in Deprived Society, 1984, p. 14.

26. Ibid., p. 693.

27. Sharma, A.K., Chairman, Editorial Board, Fifth Survey of Educational Research, 1997, p. 372.
28. Ibid., p. 372.
29. Buch, Fourth Survey, op.cit., p. 697.
30. Ibid., p. 709.
31. John Babu, CH, Rajendra Prasad, T.J., Madhukar, G.M. and Bhaskara Roa, D., Problem Solving in Mathematics, op.cit., p. 65.
32. Sridevi. C., A Comparative Study of the Achievement in Mathematics and Educational Aspirations of Intermediate Students Studying in Residential and Non - Residential Junior Colleges, Dissertation, 1991, p. 108.
33. Soujanya Meri, C., A Study of the Relationship between Mathematical Interest and Academic Achievement in Mathematics of IX class Pupils in Guntur City, Dissertation, 2000, p. 57.
34. Buch, Fourth Survey, op.cit., p. 809.
35. Ibid., p. 836.
36. Ibid., p. 845.
37. Buch, Third Survey, op.cit., p. 658.
38. Ibid., p. 663.
39. Ibid., p. 682.
40. Buch, Fourth Survey, op.cit., p. 857.
41. Buch, Fourth Survey, op.cit., p. 867.
42. Ibid., p. 1430.
43. Ibid., p. 7.
44. Tiwari, A.N., Achievement Motivation in Deprived Society, op.cit., p. 14.

45. Pillai, J.K., Effective Teaching, Madhurai Kamaraj University, 1999, p. 99.

46. Papalia, D.E. and Sally, W. Olds, Psychology, 1987, pp. 334-337.

47. Tiwari, A.N., Achievement Motivation in Deprived Society, op.cit., pp 6-7.

48. Tiwari, A.N., Achievement Motivation in Deprived Society, op.cit., pp. 9-10.

3

Methodology

Overview

This chapter deals with the methodology of the study. It consists of eight sections. The first one gives an overview of the entire chapter. The second outlines the problem of the study, and the objectives, operational definitions of the key words and variables of the study are outlined. The third section briefly describes the hypotheses. The fourth and fifth sections explain the basic assumptions and delimitations of the study. The sixth section describes the population and the sample of the study. The seventh one describes the tools of the study. The final section is the documentary notes citing references made in the chapter.

The Problem of the Study

Problem Stated

The statement of the problem either in question form or as a declarative statement attempts to focus on a goal and thereby gives direction to the research problem[1]. It must be limited enough in scope to make a definite conclusion possible. A problem suggests a specific answer or conclusion. It is in this line of thought that the problem of the study is stated as under

A Study of the Achievement Motivation and Achievement in Mathematics of APSWR School Students

Objectives of the Study

The following objectives were framed for the present research study.

1. To find out the level of achievement motivation possessed by the students of APSWR schools.
2. To find out the level of achievement in mathematics possessed by the students of APSWR schools.
3. To identify the association between achievement motivation and achievement in mathematics of APSWR schools.
4. To compare the achievement motivation and achievement in mathematics of boys and girls of APSWR schools.
5. To compare the achievement motivation and achievement in mathematics of rural and urban APSWR school students.
6. To compare the achievement motivation and achievement in mathematics of SC and OBC students of APSWR schools.
7. To find out the association between achievement motivation and achievement in mathematics in APSWR school students.
8. To find out the association between achievement motivation and achievement in mathematics of boys and girls of APSWR schools.
9. To find out the association between achievement motivation and achievement in mathematics of the students of rural and urban APSWR school students.
10. To find out the association between achievement motivation and achievement in mathematics of SC and OBC students of APSWR schools.

Operational Definitions of the Key Terms

The operational definitions of the important terms used in the present study are discussed and defined here with.

Achievement Motivation

The basis of achievement motivation is achievement motive, that is the motive to achieve[2]. Those who engage themselves in a task on account of an achievement motive are said to work under the spirit of achievement motivation. The desire to improve his performance at school or to get a good grade or to become an engineer and so on is known as achievement motive. The theory of achievement motivation was developed by McClelland and his associates in 1951 at the University of Harward. He defined motive as "A reintegration of a change in a fact by a cue and anticipation of a future change in affect contigent upon certain actions".[3] The first term, of two important terms in the definition, is reintegration which means reinstatement of psychological process in the conscious as a result of the stimulation by an environment event; and second is cue which is the cause of affect in arousal in the individual. Achievement motive may be considered as a disposition to approach success or a capacity for taking pride in accomplishment when success at one or another activity is achieved.

Achievement motivation is expectancy of finding satisfaction in mastery of difficult and challenging performances. Whereas in the field of education in particular it stands for the pursuit of excellence. The person, who is more motivated to achieve, tries to maximize his own anxiety about failure, struggle hard for getting success and derive maximum pleasure from success.

Achievement Motivation Scale

Various attempts have been made to derive some measures for the measurement of achievement motivation. There are two main categories : [4] 1. Achievement Motivation Scales, and 2. T.A.T. Type Instruments.

Achievement motivation scales have been constructed on the pattern of attitude motivation scales. Various such scales are now available. The investigator taken for use Achievement Motivation Scale of Dr. Shah Beena.

There are 40 partly completed sentences in this test. Each sentence can be completed meaningfully, if one links it up with any one of the alternatives offered. The task is to select only one answer which seems to correspond most with one's present feelings and then put a tick mark (✓) against the selected alternative. All the items in the test have to be answered. The following is one illustration of them numbered serially as 31st in this scale.

31. I feel proud of those friends who. . . . .

A. achieve pass marks in examination.

B. provide help to weaker students.

C. get brilliant success in examination.

In the present study, the Achievement Motivation Scale (A.M.S) was employed to study the achievement motivation of APSWR school students. With the responses of the testees it is tried to have an idea of the relative level of achievement motivation.

Achievement in Mathematics

The subject mathematics plays an important role in the school curriculum to develop thinking, reasoning and problem solving abilities of pupils which will inturn enable them to become good citizens of the present cybernetic world. The assessment or the attainment in the subject is also very important to sort the students into different categories and to encourage them to study the subject effectively and to field remedial measures for all types of disorders in the subject.

Freeman (1965) defines a test of educational achievement as a test designed to measure knowledge, understanding, skills in a specified subject or group of subjects[5]. Thus, according to him, an educational achievement test measures an individual's knowledge and understanding or skills in a particular branch of knowledge. The standardized achievement tests are used to determine the degree of achievement in a specific subject matter. Achievement tests attempt to measure what an individual has learned - his or her present level of performance. An achievement test is also used for purposes of guidance and counselling. It has found useful in remedial teaching programmes as well as in determining the class to which a student should be admitted into. Frequently, achievement test scores are used in evaluating the influences of courses of study, teachers' teaching method and other factors considered to be significant in educational practice.

The achievement in mathematics is the performance of the students in mathematics in an examination.

APSWR Schools

In residential schools, students stay in the school campus with their teachers instead of coming daily from their houses. So, they spend all their time either on the school premises or in the hostels and pursue studies under the constant supervision of teachers. Such schools were considered as residential schools.

In accordance with the guidance given by the Constitution of India, Government of Andhra Pradesh used the residential schools as an innovative modern tool to provide standard education. In Andhra Pradesh, there are three types of residential schools and each set of schools are lead by Educational, Social Welfare and Tribal Welfare ministries with their separate and administrative autonomous bodies such as APREIS, APSWREIS and APTWREIS.

APSWREI Society is started with an aim to provide complete modern education to the scheduled caste children. With the help of Andhra Pradesh government, this society started several schools to provide modern education for boys and girls of scheduled caste category. In 1983-84, there were 46 institutions. At present (2002) there are 165 high schools, 118 Junior. Colleges, 4 ITIs, 3 polytechnic colleges and 5 B.C.A colleges throughout the state and are meeting the requirements of scheduled caste students.

The schools, which are run by this society are referred to as APSWR schools.

Children of SC and OBC Categories

The Education Commission (1964-66) stressed the need for providing equality of educational opportunities to all sections of the population belonging to different castes, regions and religions. Equalisation of educational opportunity means providing suitable education for all in accordance with their interest, abilities and attitudes. The modern trend in the social change is towards the establishment of equality, freedom, justice and fraternity in the social order. The terms 'Scheduled Caste' and 'Scheduled Tribes' are used mainly in the context of Indian society.

The problems of the children from these communities are interwoven each being a cause and effect of the other. For example, when the occupation of the family is menial, it does not fetch adequate wages and low wages lead to poverty. This poverty often becomes the cause of illhealth, malnutrition, inferior surroundings or habitats. Parents of these children were also born in these conditions. They did not have access to schooling and education. The children of such houses have to earn their livings from very young age. Naturally, they cannot go to school and so they remain illiterate. Thus, the awareness that comes with formed schooling and the job opportunities available for literates are denied to them and inturn to their children. Some children have to work for longer hours and they cannot go to schools. Many children live in villages and they do not have convenient schools.

Under these circumstances, the Government of A.P., under the supervision of the Social Welfare Ministry, is providing the opportunity of better educational facilities through APSWR schools. These schools are providing education for the children of scheduled castes and other backward classes covering H.C. (Harizan Christian), S. T. (Scheduled Tribe), B. C. (Backward Classes) and O. C. (Other Caste) with Gurukula Education System.

In each section of every class of APSWR school, not more than 40 admissions will be made. Out of 40 seats, 30 (75%) seats are allotted for scheduled caste students and 10 seats (25%) are allotted for students of other backward classes, namely, H.C., S.T., B.C and O.C.

Urban and Rural Schools

The schools located in an urban area were considered as urban schools. An urban area should satisfy the following conditions [6].

1. It should have a municipal corporation, cantonment board, notified town area committee, etc.

2. It should have a minimum population of five thousand.
3. Atleast 75% of its male working population should be engaged in non-agricultural pursuits.
4. It should have a population of atleast 400 persons per square kilometer.

The schools located in rural area were considered as rural schools. A rural area should have a population below five thousand with 75% of the population engaged in agricultural pursuits.

Variables of the Study

The variables considered for the present study are

3.24.1. Boys versus Girls

3.24.2. Rural APSWR school students versus Urban APSWR school students

3.24.3. SC Students versus OBC Students.

The rationale for choosing the above stated variables is discussed herewith.

Boys versus Girls

Sex was taken as a variable to see if there is any significant difference between boys and girls in possessing achievement motivation and achievement in mathematics.

In olden days, the boys were educated and the girls were restricted to their kitchens by their adult community. Times changed and the adults recognised the importance of women education. In the words of our Late Prime Minister Pandit Jawaharlal Nehru[7], "If you educate a man, you educate only one person; If you educate a woman, you educate the entire family." In the course of time, women's education gained importance and many parents are encouraging their daughters to pursue higher education and even allowing them to go abroad. The women are also showing excellence in all fields. Their presence is felt almost in all fields.

As the physiological conditions, exposure to society, education and other aspects of girls and boys vary differently, there may be a significant difference in the possession of achievement motivation and achievement in mathematics. The boys may be exposed to the society to a larger extent, but the girls spend most of their time either in going through books or helping their parents at home. These factors will show their influence on motivation and achievement.

It is especially important to study the level of possession of achievement motivation and achievement in mathematics of APSWR school students because they just enter the adolescent stage, which is otherwise known as the period of stress and strain. At this stage, this sample finds it extremely difficult to adjust themselves in the society because they are accepted neither as adults nor as children. It is also familiar that girls mature faster than boys at the early adolescent stage, both physically and mentally. The above factors will also have their own impact on the possession of achievement motivation and achievement in mathematics.

So, a comparison between boys and girls will reveal of any difference that exists in the possession of achievement motivation and achievement in mathematics.

Rural APSWR school students versus Urban APSWR school students

Generally, the urban schools are well equipped in many aspects when compared with the rural schools. The buildings, the libraries, the laboratories, the teaching staff, the educational atmosphere, the competitive spirit among the pupils, the amenities provided to pupils to pursue education, the exposure to science fairs and exhibitions, the student participation in teaching-learning process, the use of audio-visual aids, etc., will always be better in urban schools than in rural schools. Though the rural and urban APSWR schools have equal level of amenities, facilities and other benefits, the attitude of teachers and students have their own impact on motivation and achievement. The atmosphere of rural APSWR schools is pure naturalistic without any pollution, disturbances, and with healthy atmosphere.

A comparision between rural and urban school students will bring out the difference in the level of possession of achievement motivation and achievement in mathematics, if there is any.

SC students versus OBC students

In APSWR schools, students will be admitted on the basis of entrance examination marks. Admission will be given for the students whose fathers' annual income is below Rs. 18,000/-. Special privilege and priority in admission will be given for the children from the families of first generation learners, agricultural labourers (farm-hands), joginies, scavengers and bonded labourers in the order of preference. The students include SCs (75%) and OBCs (25%).

A comparison between the students SC and OBC categories will bring out the difference in the level of achievement motivation and achievement in mathematics, if there is any.

Hypotheses of the Study

The hypothesis is a tentative answer to a question. It is a hunch or an educated guess, to be subjected to the process of verification or disconfirmation[8]. Hypotheses are suggested problem solutions which are expressed as generalizations or propositions. They are the statements consisting of elements expressed in an orderly system of relationships which seek to describe or to explain events that have not yet been confirmed by facts. They may provide the conceptual elements that complete the known data, conceptual relationships that systematize unordered elements or conceptual meanings and interpretations that explain the unknown phenomena. By logically relating known facts intelligent guesses about unknown conditions can be made. The hypotheses are able to extend and enlarge our knowledge.

Best identifies the following four basic characteristics of a good hypothesis[9].

— it should be reasonable.

— it should be consistent with known facts or theories.

— it should be stated in such a way that it can be tested and found to be probably true or probably false.

— it should be stated in the simplest possible terms.

With these criteria as a frame of reference, the following working hypotheses were formulated for the present study.

The three major hypotheses and their rationale have been discussed. Each one of the main hypothesis has been studied in further detail by forming three sub-hypotheses under each head.

Hypothesis 1

APSWR school students are possessing high achievement motivation.

Motivation is one of the most important conditions of learning. A high degree of motivation helps in arousing students into action and ensuring active participation in learning activities. The teacher has to direct the learning process and must be aware of the nature of important motives. Development of achievement motive is affected by a number of variables in home, school and society. Home plays an important role in the early training of children for the development of attitudes and motives. Parental expectation and guidance to the child develop need for high achievement in life. The society and its social philosophy is an important variable in developing achievement motive. There are communities which are achievement-oriented.

Before coming to school, the child gathers many experiences which become an integral part of his personality and form his attitude towards life. But even then, the school helps a lot to sharpen already acquired experiences and develops positive attitudes in children. The teacher can play a very crucial role in the development of achievement motive by following the following methods[10] : 1. The teacher should make clear the importance of achievement motive in life by means of telling the stories of great men and their achievements from all walks of life. When the students are convinced in advance to believe that they would or should develop achievement motive, the efforts of the teacher will succeed. 2. The teacher should provide proper environment in the class and outside the class. The teacher's attitude and enthusiasm will create better environment for the development of achievement motive in children. 3. The teacher will succeed in his attempt if he convinces the students that developing a new motive is realistic and reasonable. 4. The teacher should relate the motive with future life of the students and assign independent responsibility to them. 5. The teacher should make clear to the students that the new motive will improve their self-image. 6. The teacher should emphasize upon the fact that new motive is an improvement on prevailing cultural values. 7. The teacher should make students committed in achieving concrete goals in life related to the newly developed motive. 8. The teacher should ask the students to keep the record of their progress towards their goal. 9. Self-study should be emphasized. 10. The teacher should make an effort to develop conducive social climate in the class so that every individual should feel that he belongs to a group.

As stated earlier, under the area of achievement motivation, the variables namely sex, rural versus urban, SC versus OBC students were considered. To study each of these variables in detail, the following sub-hypotheses were formulated. They were stated in Directional Hypothesis form.

Hypothesis 1A

There is a significant difference in the level of achievement motivation possessed by boys and girls of APSWR schools.

Hypothesis 1B

There is a significant difference in the level of achievement motivation possessed by the students of rural and urban APSWR schools.

Hypothesis 1C

There is a significant difference in the level of achievement motivation possessed by the SC and OBC students of APSWR schools.

Hypothesis 2

APSWR school students are possessing high achievement in mathematics

Achievement is a paramount importance, particularly in the present socio-economic and cultural contexts, and great emphasis is placed on achievement right from the beginning of the formal education. It is a task-oriented behaviour that allows the individual's performance to be evaluated according to some internally or externally imposed criterion, that involves some standard of excellence.[11]

Achievement is related to the acquisition of principles and generalizations and the capacity to perform efficiently certain manipulations of objects, symbols and ideas. Assessment of achievement has been largely confirmed to the evaluation in terms of knowledge and understanding. It is universally accepted that the acquisition of factual data is not an end in itself but that an individual who has received education should show the evidence of having understood them. But, for obvious reasons, the examinations are largely confined to the measurement of the amount of information acquired by the students.

Achievement in terms of subject matter is conventionally assured in our institutions by employing a system of marks or grades and it has been strongly argued that marks are necessary for effective teaching-learning. Marks also set goals and motivate the students. It is universally accepted that marks serve as the basis of classification and certification.

The students studying in residential schools stay round the clock in school campus and they will be under a strict vigilance of the teachers. The students go through the lesson regularly and get their doubts clarified. The resident teachers also check the student's performance continuously and at the same time these schools will have well equipped laboratories, libraries and other centres of learning. As stated earlier under this area, the variables, namely, boys versus girls; rural versus urban students and SC and OBC students were considered. Under the achievement in mathematics, the following three sub-hypotheses were framed.

Hypothesis 2A

There is a significant difference in the level of achievement in mathematics possessed by boys and girls of APSWR schools.

Hypothesis 2B

There is a significant difference in the level of achievement in mathematics possessed by the students of rural and urban APSWR schools.

Hypothesis 2C

There is a significant difference in the level of achievement in mathematics possessed by the SC and OBC students of APSWR schools.

Hypothesis 3

There is a significant association between achievement motivation and achievement in mathematics in APSWR school students.

Many studies indicate a relationship between achievement motivation and achievement in mathematics. Suitable suggestions may be placed before the teachers and planners if there is an association between these two for helping the students in achieving excellency in academic endeavours.

Under the area of association between achievement motivation and achievement in mathematics of APSWR school students, the following three sub- hypotheses were framed.

Hypothesis 3A

There is a significant significant association between achievement motivation and achievement in mathematics of boys and girls of APSWR schools.

Hypothesis 3B

There is a significant association between achievement motivation and achievement in mathematics of the students of rural and urban APSWR schools.

Hypothesis. 3C

There is a significant association between achievement motivation and achievement in mathematics of SC and OBC students of APSWR schools.

Assumptions of the Study

Achievement motivation may be distributed normally in the students of APSWR Schools.

Achievement in mathematics may be normal in the students studying in the APSWR Schools.

The achievement motivation and achievement in mathematics may have association between them.

Delimitations of the Study

The study is limited to the APSWR schools located in south coastal area of Andhra Pradesh, which covers GUNTUR, PRAKASAM and NELLORE districts; that is the 3rd zone of Andhra Pradesh. The study is further limited to Xth class students of twelve selected APSWR schools, selected equally from rural and urban areas. The study is also limited to SC and OBC students who are studying in APSWR schools only.

Population and Sample

A population is any group of individuals that have one or more characteristics in common. The population may be all the individuals of a particular type or a more restricted part of that group. A sample is a small proportion of a population selected for observation and analysis. By observing the characteristics of the sample, one can make certain inferences about the characteristics of the population from which it is drawn.[12]

The students studying Xth class in the APSWR schools will be the population of the study. Out of the total population, a representative sample of 480 students will be selected using stratified random sampling technique. Details of sample selection is given here under.

After finalizing the variables of the present study, consideration was given to whether the entire population is to be made the subject for data collection or a particular group is to be selected as representative of the whole population. The 'entire population' here refers to all the tenth class students of the APSWR schools of Andhra Pradesh. Of the two techniques, the second one namely the selection of a group as a representative of the whole population was found to be more convenient and suitable. This technique leads to a considerable saving of time, effort and finance. The number of students selected is small, and so it is possible to make a detailed and intensive study. This generally leads to more accurate and reliable results. As this sampling technique has may advantages, it was selected for the collection of data. Sampling is simply the process of learning about the population on the basis of a sample drawn from it.[13]

In any social research, various methods are utilised for selection and drawing of samples. After a detailed study of all these methods and considering the variables selected for the research work, the stratified sampling method was found to be most suitable.

In the stratified sampling method, the entire population is divided into smaller homogeneous groups (Best) [14] or strata, and then the sample is selected with in each group. Every sampling unit in the population is placed in one of the strata prior to the selection of the sample so that the sum of the strata is identical with the population.

Stratified sampling method has certain merits and advantages as a technique of sampling. Auckof has rightly said that 'stratified sampling enables the researcher to make a comparision of properties of the strata as well as to estimate population characteristics' (Kerlinger, 1964).[15]

In the stratified sampling method, the investigator has greater control over the selection of the sample when compared with random sampling. In random sampling, although every group has a chance of being selected and included in the sample, there is every possibility and some times it does happen that certain important groups are left unrepresented. But in stratified sampling method, no important group is likely to be left out.

Stratified sampling method is the ideal one when comparison between different variables has to be made. For example, if comparison has to be made between boys and girls or rural and urban pupils, it would be very difficult to select the required number of units through any other method of sampling. If any other method is used, the problem of bias and prejudice creeps in.

Replacement of units is also possible in the stratified sampling method. Normally, if a particular unit is not accessible for a study, it is difficult to replace it by another, but in this method it is possible. Stephen states that 'stratification automatically brings about a replacement of persons lost to the sample, by persons of the same stratum, thus partly correcting the bias that would result if there were no replacement of losses. As the entire population is divided into particular strata, it is easy and convenient to replace an inaccessible case by an accessible one.

The purposes of stratification is to increase the efficiency of sampling by dividing a heterogeneous universe in such a way that (i) there is as great homogeneity as possible with in each stratum and (ii) as marked a difference as possible between the strata.[16]

In this stratified sampling method, much depends on the stratification process. The following precautions were taken while stratifying the population : the variables involved in the study were taken note of; care was taken to see that each stratum in the universe was large enough in size so that selection of items could be done on random basis; the strata formed were definite and clear cut; each stratum was free from influence of the other; that there was no overlapping.

Before actually selecting the sample, certain fundamental principles were considered to make the sample scientific and clear-cut.

Firstly, the 'universe' was clearly defined. In the technical phraseology of research, the whole population out of which the samples are selected is known as the 'universe'. For the present research work, the universe includes all the students of tenth class studying in APSWR schools of Andhra Pradesh. The study was limited to a particular geographical area to facilitate appropriate sample selection.

According to the second principle, decision has to be made about the units of the sample. A unit of sample may be a house, a family, a group of individuals or a single individual. A good unit should possess the following characteristics.[17] (A) Clarity : The unit should be clearly defined in unambiguous terms. This would make the study easy and efficient. For the present research work, a sampling unit was defined as a student of tenth class studying in any APSWR school of Andhra Pradesh. (B) Suitability : A good unit should be well suited to the problem under study. Since the problem is the possession and comparison of achievement motivation and achievement in mathematics of the tenth class students of APSWR schools of Andhra Pradesh, the unit selected is well suited to the problem. (C) Accessibility : The unit selected should be easily accessible to the researcher. If the units selected are difficult to researcher and if he fails to make use of them, the study would be vitiated. The selected sampling unit, i. e., a tenth class student is easily accessible since he/she could be approached in any APSWR school.

Besides considering these principles, it is extremely important to think about the size of the sample to be selected. If the sample is either too small or too large, it will make the study difficult and also make the results untenable. According to Parten, an optimum sample in survey is one which fulfils the requirements of effective representativeness, reliability and flexibility. The sample should be small enough to avoid intolerable sampling error. The size of sample for the present research work was decided after considering the following factors.

Since an intensive study was planned, a very large number of samples were not selected. In case of an intensive study, very large number of samples are not so useful as they involve huge consumption of the resources. A smaller sample is convenient.

The size and selection of the samples will also be influenced by the nature of the universe. If the universe is homogenous, even a small-sized sample may yield dependable and required results. If the universe is heterogenous, small-sized samples may not be useful. In case of the present study, the heterogenous universe was spilt into smaller homogenous groups and the samples were selected from these strata. For example, all the tenth class students were broadly grouped under boys and girls. A sample was selected from each of these two groups.

The investigator needs to determine the number of the groups to be formed. In case the number of groups proposed is large, the size of the samples shall have to be large so that every group should be proper in size and suit to the requirements of the study. In case the number of groups proposed is small, even small-sized samples can fulfil the requirement. In the case of the present study, the number of groups into which the universe was divided are girls and boys, rural and urban, SC and OBC students. Since the number of groups are moderate, a reasonably large sample was selected from each of these groups.

Practical considerations and accuracy will also play a vital role in determining the size of the sample. Every study is guided by certain practical considerations such as time, resources, accessibility of data, etc. Generally, it is believed that a large-sized sample is more representative and generally produces accurate results. This, of course, depends upon the technique of sampling used. If the technique is scientific, even small-sized samples can produce dependable and accurate results. While selecting the size of the sample for the present study, practical considerations like the availability of resources and time were taken into consideration. Care was taken to make the sample selection technique as scientific as possible.

The size of the sample is also governed by the size of the tools to be used. In case the tools are short and the questions asked pertain to certain limited factors, a large sample can be selected. In case the tools are large and the questions complicated, the sample should be small in size so that, from administrative point of view, the investigator may not be put to unnecessary troubles. In the present study, the tool was quite elaborate, hence a very large sample was not selected.

The sampling method also determines the size of the sample. When random sampling method is used, the samples have to be large. On the other hand, if samples are selected through stratified sampling method, the reliability can be achieved even with the help of the small-sized samples.

After taking into consideration all these factors which influence the size of the sample, it was decided that an ideal sample would consist of 480 students. This sample is small enough to avoid unnecessary expenditure and large enough to avoid intolerable sampling errors.

After deciding about the sampling method and the size of the sample, the universe selected was divided into different strata. The variables chosen for the study were considered to divide the universe. The variables chosen were :

1. Boys vs girls
2. Rural vs urban students
3. SC and OBC students

Following the sampling procedure, 480 Xth class students were selected as sample for this study. Out of these 480 students, 240 were from rural and 240 were from urban APSWR schools, and out of 480 students, 240 were boys and 240 were girls. As per reservation in the admission made by the Government of Andhra Pradesh, 360 SC and 120 OBC students were selected.

Table - 3.1

Distribution of Sample

Total Xth class Students

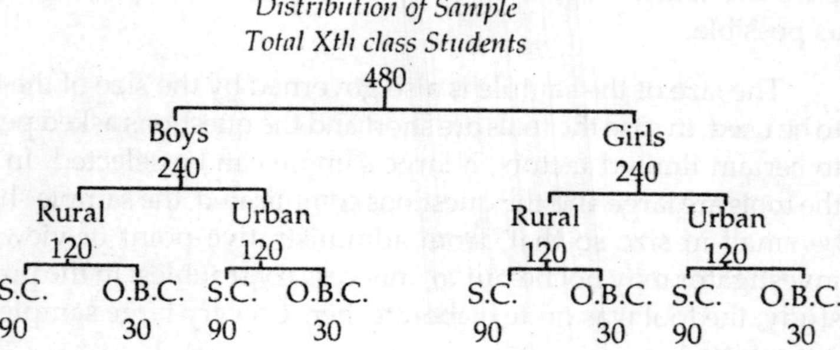

The total sample includes - rural students 240, urban students 240, boys - 240, girls - 240; SC students - 360, and OBC students 120. The sampling design employed involved not only the stratification of the universe but also random sampling technique to select samples from within the stratum.

Tools of the Study

A research tool plays a major role in any worthwhile research as it is the sole factor in determining the sound data and in arriving at perfect conclusions about the problem or study in hand, which, ultimately, helps in providing suitable remedial measures to the problem concerned.

A great variety of research tools has been developed to aid in the acquisition of data. These tools are of many kinds and employ distinctive ways of describing and quantifying data. Each tool is particularly appropriate for certain sources of data, yielding information of the kind and in the form that would be most effectively used, like the tools in the carpenter's chest, each is appropriate in a given situation.[18]

The selection and use of tools can be done in two ways.[19] The first one is to construct a tool independently by the investigator for his own study. Here, there are many problems in doing so. Preparation and standardization of a perfect tool itself is a major task, and one can easily say that it is a doctoral study itself. On construction of their own tools, Anand and Padma (1987) felt that 'A note of caution has to be struck when a researcher develops a tool for his study by merely pooling up some items and does not subject it to the sophisticated techniques of tool construction. The result would be then, obviously, a poor quality research. With this, one can say that preparation and standardization of tools is a major task, and one should take care in aspects like selection of area and sample, pooling up of statements related to the area and sample, consulting the experts, and application of sophisticated statistical techniques.

The second way of selection and use of tools is right selection of tools from already standardized ones available in the field of study. Here also it involves a tedious job in locating the tools and identifying their usefulness to the study on hand. Even then, this technique is very useful when a research work is taken to study in depth and when the research work involves a good number of variables. Some people believe that some of the instruments available do not measure up to their standards. Hence new ones. In some instances, consideration should be given to the logistics of the situation. Lacking time and financial resources, many researchers cannot expect to produce a better instrument. In these cases, the most logical procedure that one can follow is to choose the best instrument available for his purpose (Pearl, 1974).

Considering the flaws and merits of the selection of tools in either way, the investigator was interested in using the standardized tools as the present study involves a thorough study of achievement motivation and achievement in mathematics of APSWR school students and their association with each other.

Measurement of Achievement Motivation

After a thorough survey of literature, the investigator used the Achievement Motivation Scale (AMS) constructed and standardized by Dr. Shah Beena, Garhwal University, Srinagar, (Garhwal) which is published by Agra Psychological Research Cell, Agra.

Measurement of Achievement in Mathematics

To measure the achievement in mathematics, marks of mathematics obtained in the term-end examination, that is the quarterly examination. The reason for taking these marks is that this examination is the immediate examination after conducting Achievement Motivation Scale.

Documentation

1. John W. Best., Research in Education, 1977, p. 25.
2. Mangal, S.K., Educational Psychology, 1998, p. 198.
3. Chauhan, S.S., Advanced Educational Psychology, 1978, p. 219.
4. Mangal., op.cit., p. 200.
5. Best, op.cit., p. 193.
6. Bhaskara Rao, D., Scientific Attitude VIS-A-VIS Scientific

Aptitude, 1996, p.44.

7. Ibid., p. 45.

8. Best, op.cit., p. 39.

9. Ibid., p. 39.

10. Chauhan, op.cit., pp. 220-221.

11. Kuppuswamy, B., Advanced Educational Psychology, 1964, p. 176.

12. Best, op.cit., pp. 8-9.

13. Gupta, S.P., Statistical Methods, 1980, p. E - 4.3.

14. Best, op.cit., p. 12.

15. Bhaskara Rao, D, op.cit., p. 53.

16. Gupta, op.cit., p. E - 4.10.

17. Bhaskara Rao, D, op.cit., p. 53.

18. Best, J.W., Research in Education, 1977, p. 156.

19. Bhaskara Rao, D, op.cit., p. 59.

4

Data Analysis

Overview

This chapter deals with the analysis of data collected for the study. It consists of six sections. This first one gives an overview of the entire chapter. The second one relates to the introduction for the topic. The third section is the analysis of the level of achievement motivation of the whole sample and variables. The fourth section is the analysis of the level of achievement in mathematics of the total sample and variables. The fifth section is the analysis of the association of achievement motivation and achievement in mathematics of the whole sample and the variables. The final section furnishes the documentary notes.

Introduction

The next steps in the process of research after the collection of data are the organization, analysis and interpretation of data and formulation of conclusions and generalizations to get a meaningful picture out of the raw information collected. The analysis and interpretation of data involve the objective material in the possession of the researcher and his subjective reactions and desires to be derived from the data the inherent meaning in their relation to the problem[1].

The mass data collected through the use of various tools need to be systematized and organized, i.e., edited, classified and tabulated before it can serve the purpose. Here, editing implies the checking of gathered data for accuracy, utility and completeness; classifying refers to the dividing of the information into different categories, classes or heads for use; and tabulation denotes the recording of the classified material in accurate mathematical terms, eg., marking and counting frequency tallies for different items on which information is gathered.

Analysis of data means studying the tabulated material in order to determine inherent facts or meanings. It involves breaking down the existing complex factors into simpler parts and putting the parts together in new arrangements for purposes of interpretation.

This present chapter, Analysis of Data, hence, includes a study of different techniques adopted for analysis and interpretation of data, and the results that resulted from the analysis of data.

After finalizing the tools and sample of the study, the data was collected from four hundred eighty students studying tenth class. Achievement Motivation Scale of Dr. Shah Beena was used to identify the level of achievement motivation of the sample. The mathematics marks obtained in Quarterly examination were taken to study the level of achievement in mathematics. After the collection of data was finished, it was analysed keeping the objectives and hypotheses of the study in view. The analysis of data was carried out in the following manner.

As mentioned earlier in the previous chapters, the study included three major aspects, viz, achievement motivation, achievement in mathematics and the association between these two. From the tool and term-end examination, the total scores of achievement motivation and achievement in mathematics were taken as raw scores for each candidate. This raw data was put to statistical treatment. Each of the different aspects, viz, achievement motivation and achievement in mathematics of the study was taken first into consideration individually. Later, these two aspects were tested for their inter-relationship. The hypotheses framed were statistically tested and accordingly accepted or rejected.

Achievement Motivation

The total score of achievement motivation of each student was taken to find out the level of achievement motivation possessed by each sub-sample as well as the total sample of the study. The maximum score that a student can get is 120 and the minimum is 40. In the present study, the highest score secured by a student was 120 and the lowest was 69.

For the purpose of classification of the level of achievement motivation possessed by the sample and sub-samples, the level of achievement motivation was categorized[2] by using the normal probability distribution. The achievement motivation level of the total sample and sub-samples was classified into three categories, viz, low, average and high.

Table 4.1

Division of whole sample and sub-samples into Low, Average and High Groups

Sample/ Sub Sample	Sample Size	Mean	Standard Deviation	Low Level	Average Level	High Level
Whole	480	96.40	6.46	40 - 90	91 - 102	103 - 120
Boys	240	95.78	6.66	40 - 89	90 - 101	102 - 120
Girls	240	97.02	6.22	40 - 91	92 - 102	103 - 120
Rural	240	96.86	6.66	40 - 90	91 - 101	102 - 120
Urban	240	95.93	6.25	40 - 90	91 - 103	104 - 120
SC	360	96.07	6.47	40 - 90	91 - 102	103 - 120
OBC	120	97.38	6.37	40 - 91	92 - 103	104 - 120

The mean scores were used to identify the level[3] of achievement motivation possessed by the APSWR school students and to compare the sub-sample variation. The values of standard deviation were used to measure the spread or dispersion of scores in distribution[4]. The critical ratios[5] were calculated to test the significant difference in the means of the two sub-samples of each variable. The research hypotheses formulated for this study were accordingly accepted or rejected.

The chi-square test of independence was applied for comparing the experimentally obtained results with those of to be expected theoretically on some hypothesis[6].

Hypothesis 1

"APSWR school students are possessing high achievement motivation."

To test the validity of the hypothesis, the total scores of all the sample were calculated to arrive at mean and standard deviation of the sample. The results are as follows.

Table 4.2

Levels of achievement motivation of the whole sample

Sample	Mean	Standard Deviation
480	96.40	6.46

The students studying in APSWR schools are holding average level of achievement motivation. In the sample, as per the standard deviation, there is lower dispersion of scores in the units of sample.

The chi-square (χ^2) test of independence was applied to test the divergence of observed results from those expected on the hypothesis of equal probability of distribution of a trait in the sample.

Table 4.3

Distribution of achievement motivation in the whole sample

Sample		Low	Average	High	χ^2
480	f_0	96	318	66	6.88*
	f_e	76	328	76	

df=2 ** Not significant at 0.01 level.*

ρ at 0.01 level is 9.21

Fo = frequency of occurrence of observed or experimentally determined facts.

Fe = frequency of occurrence expected on some hypothesis.

It is clear from table 4.3 that the distribution of achievement motivation in the whole sample is normal.

The hypothesis that the "APSWR school students are possessing high achievement motivation" can be rejected as the students hold an average achievement motivation.

Hypothesis 1A

"There is a significant difference in the level of achievement motivation possessed by boys and girls of APSWR schools."

A comparision of the achievement motivation scores of boys and girls was made to find out the difference in the level of achievement motivation possessed by them. The data are as follows.

Table 4.4

Comparision of achievement motivation of boys and girls

Variable	Sample	Mean	Standard deviation	Mean difference	Critical ratio
Boys	240	95.78	6.66	1.24	2.10*
Girls	240	97.02	6.22		

ρ at 0.01 level is 2.59 ** Not significant at 0.01 level.*

From table 4.4, it can be seen that boys and girls of APSWR schools hold average achievement motivation. It can also be seen clearly that there is no significant difference in the level of achievement motivation possessed by boys and girls as critical the ratio value is not significant. The standard deviation indicates that the divergence is low both in boys and girls.

As the critical ratio is not significant it can be said that the little difference that exists may be due to sampling error.

Further, the chi-square test was applied to test the divergence of observed results of boys and girls from those expected on the hypothesis of equal probability. The chi-square values were calculated for each sub-sample and are given below in Table 4.5.

Table 4.5

Distribution of achievement motivation in boys and girls

Variable	Sample		Low	Average	High	χ^2
Boys	240	f_0	40	157	43	1.07*
		f_e	38	164	38	
Girls	240	f_0	49	156	35	3.81*
		f_e	38	164	38	

df=2 * *Not significant at 0.01 level.*

ρ at 0.01 level is 9.21

As can be seen from the above table, it can be concluded that the achievement motivation is distributed normally in both boys and girls.

The hypothesis that "there is a significant difference in the level of achievement motivation possessed by boys and girls of APSWR schools" can be rejected.

Hypothesis 1B

"There is a significant difference in the level of achievement motivation possessed by the students of rural and urban APSWR schools."

A comparision was made to identify the difference in the possession of achievement motivation by the students of rural and urban APSWR schools.

Table 4.6

Comparision of achievement motivation of the students of rural and urban APSWR schools

Variable	Sample	Mean	Standard deviation	Mean difference	Critical ratio
Rural	240	96.86	6.66	0.93	1.58*
Urban	240	95.93	6.25		

**Not significant at 0.01 level.*

As can be seen from table 4.6, there is no significant difference in the level of achievement motivation possessed by the tenth class students of rural and urban APSWR schools. Both the rural and urban APSWR schools students fall under average achievement motivation category.

The chi-square test values of the students studying in rural and urban APSWR schools are as follows.

Table 4.7

Distribution of achievement motivation in the students of rural and urban APSWR schools

Variable	Sample		Low	Average	High	χ^2
		f_0	45	152	43	
Rural	240					2.54*
		f_e	38	164	38	
		f_0	40	171	29	
Urban	240					2.83*
		f_e	38	164	38	

**Not significant at 0.01 level.*

From the above table 4.7, it is clear that the distribution of achievement motivation in various levels is normal, as both the chi-square values are not significant.

The hypothesis that "there is a significant difference in the level of achievement motivation possessed by the students of rural and urban APSWR schools" can be rejected.

Hypothesis 1C

"There is a significant difference in the level of achievement motivation possessed by the SC and OBC students of APSWR schools."

A comparision of achievement motivation scores of SC and OBC students of APSWR schools is made. The data are as follows.

Table 4.8

Comparision of achievement motivation of SC and OBC students

Variable	Sample	Mean	Standard deviation	Mean difference	Critical ratio
SC	360	96.07	6.47	1.31	1.96*
OBC	120	97.38	6.37		

**Not significant at 0.01 level.*

From table 4.8, it can be seen that SC and OBC students of APSWR schools are holding average achievement motivation. It can also be seen clearly that there is no significant difference in the level of achievement motivation possessed by both SC and OBC students as there is no significant difference in the mean scores of both cases.

The chi-square test values of SC and OBC students of APSWR schools are as follows.

Table 4.9

Distribution of achievement motivation of SC and OBC students

Variable	Sample		Low	Average	High	χ^2
SC	360	f_0	78	247	35	16.23#
		f_e	57	246	57	
OBC	120	f_0	23	78	19	1.04*
		f_e	19	82	19	

** Not significant at 0.01 level.*

 # Significant at 0.01 level.

The divergence in the distribution of achievement motivation according to table 4.9 is seen only in the SC students of APSWR schools as the chi-square value is highly significant. But the achievement motivation of OBC students of APSWR schools is not significant as it distributed normally. With regard to the acceptance or rejection, the chi-square values have no place as they are concerned with normal probable distribution.

The hypothesis that "there is a significant difference in the level of achievement motivation possessed by the SC and OBC students of APSWR schools" can be rejected.

Achievement in Mathematics

To measure the level of achievement in mathematics possessed by each sub-sample as well as whole sample of the study, the marks are taken. The maximum score that a student can get is 100 and the minimum is 0. In the present study, the highest score secured was 100 and the lowest score was 10.

For the purpose of classification of achievement in mathematics possessed by the samples, the achievement in mathematics level was categorized by applying the normal probability of distribution.

The classification of achievement in mathematics made into three categories, viz, low, average and high. The following procedure was followed.

Table 4.10

Division of whole sample and sub-samples into low, average and high groups

Sample/ Sub Sample	Sample Size	Mean	Standard Deviation	Low Level	Average Level	High Level
Whole	480	54.67	20.87	0- 34	35 - 75	76 - 100
Boys	240	54.47	21.28	0 - 33	34 - 75	76 - 100
Girls	240	54.88	20.42	0 - 34	35 - 74	75 - 100
Rural	240	53.31	21.16	0 - 32	33 - 73	74 - 100
Urban	240	56.03	20.64	0 - 35	36 - 76	77 - 100
SC	360	53.44	20.30	0 - 33	34 - 73	74 - 100
OBC	120	58.37	22.53	0 - 36	37 - 80	81 - 100

The mean scores were utilized to compare the sub-sample variation. The values of standard deviation were used to measure the dispersion of scores in each case. The chi-square test of independence was used for computing the experimentally obtained results with those to be expected theoretically on a hypothesis. The critical ratios were calculated to test the significant difference in the means of the two sub-samples of each variable. Accordingly, the research hypothesis framed for this study was accepted or rejected.

Hypothesis—2

"APSWR students are possessing high achievement in mathematics."

The validity of the above hypothesis was tested by calculating mean and standard deviation values. The results are as follows.

Table 4.11

Level of achievement in mathematics of the whole sample

Sample	Mean	Standard Deviation
480	54.67	20.87

It is evident from table 4.11 that APSWR schools students are holding average level of achievement in mathematics.

The chi-square test of independence was applied to identify the divergence in the dispersion of achievement in the sample.

Table 4.12

Distribution of achievement in mathematics in the whole sample

Sample		Low	Average	High	χ^2
480	f_0	62	330	88	4.48*
	f_e	76	328	76	

df=2 **Not significant at 0.01 level.*

p at 0.01 level is 9.21

As per the chi-square value, the distribution of achievement in mathematics in the whole sample is supporting the assumption that any psychological trait will distribute normally.

The hypothesis that "APSWR school students are possessing high achievement in mathematics" can be rejected as the students possess an average achievement in mathematics.

Hypothesis 2A

"There is a significant difference in the level of achievement in mathematics possessed by boys and girls of APSWR schools."

The data of the sub-samples were computed to test the validity of the above hypothesis. The calculations are as follows .

Table 4.13

Comparision of achievement in mathematics of boys and girls

Variable	Sample	Mean	Standard deviation	Mean difference	Critical ratio
Boys	240	54.47	21.28	0.41	0.22*
Girls	240	54.88	20.42		

ρ at 0.01 level is 2.59 ** Not significant at 0.01 level.*

From the mean scores of table 4.13, it is clear that there is no significant difference between the level of achievement in mathematics possessed by both boys and girls. This is supported by the value of critical ratio. Both the sub-samples are with average achievement in mathematics.

It is further tried to identify the distribution of achievement in mathematics in the sub-samples.

Table 4.14

Distribution of achievement in mathematics in boys and girls

Variable	Sample		Low	Average	High	χ^2
Boys	240	f_o	34	159	47	2.70*
		f_e	38	164	38	

Table Contd...

Girls	240	f_o	26	168	46	5.57*
		f_e	38	164	38	

df=2 **Not significant at 0.01 level.*

ρ at 0.01 level is 9.21

The chi-square values, according to table 4.12, of both boys and girls, indicate that the distribution of achievement in mathematics in the sub-samples is normal.

The hypothesis that "there is a significant difference in the level of achievement in mathematics possessed by boys and girls of APSWR schools" can be rejected.

Hypothesis 2B

"There is a significant difference in the level of achievement in mathematics possessed by the students of rural and urban APSWR schools."

The validity of hypothesis 2B was tested in the following manner.

Table 4.15

Comparision of achievement in mathematics of the students of rural and urban APSWR schools

Variable	Sample	Mean	Standard deviation	Mean difference	Critical ratio
Rural	240	53.31	21.16	2.72	1.42*
Urban	240	56.03	20.64		

**Not significant at 0.01 level.*

There is no difference in the level of achievement in mathematics possessed by the students studying in rural and urban APSWR schools as per the mean score values of the sub-samples. But, the urban students are relatively a little better in holding achievement in mathematics than the rural students.

Further the chi-square test was applied to identify the distribution of achievement in mathematics in the sub-samples.

Table 4.16

Distribution of achievement in mathematics in the students of rural and urban APSWR schools

Variable	Sample		Low	Average	High	χ^2
		f_0	39	159	42	
Rural	240					0.60*
		f_e	38	164	38	
		f_0	30	156	54	
Urban	240					8.81*
		f_e	38	164	38	

** Not significant at 0.01 level.*

The distribution of achievement in mathematics in the students studying in rural and urban APSWR schools is normal as the chi-square values are not significant.

The hypothesis that "there is a significant difference in the level of achievement in mathematics possessed by the students of rural and urban APSWR schools" can be rejected.

Hypothesis 2C

"There is a significant difference in the level of achievement in mathematics possessed by the SC and OBC students of APSWR schools."

The hypothesis 2C was tested for its validity by calculating mean, standard deviation and critical ratio. The data are as follows.

Table 4.17

Comparision of achievement in mathematics of the SC and OBC students

Variable	Sample	Mean	Standard deviation	Mean difference	Critical ration

Table Contd...

SC	360	53.44	20.30	4.93	2.125*
OBC	120	58.37	22.53		

**Not significant at 0.01 level.*

The mean scores, in table 4.15, indicate that there is no significant difference in the level of achievement in mathematics possessed by the SC and OBC students. The students of OBC category hold a little bit higher achievement in mathematics than those of SC students.

Further the chi-square test was applied to identify the distribution of achievement in mathematics in the sub-samples.

Table 4.18

Distribution of achievement in mathematics in the SC and OBC students of APSWR schools

Variable	Sample		Low	Average	High	χ^2
SC	360	f_0	48	243	69	3.99*
		f_e	57	246	57	
OBC	120	f_0	27	67	26	8.69*
		f_e	19	82	19	

** Not significant at 0.01 level.*

The distribution of achievement in mathematics, according to table 4.18, is not normal in both the SC and OBC students of APSWR schools as the chi-square values are not significant.

The hypothesis that "there is a significant difference in the level of achievement in mathematics possessed by the SC and OBC students of APSWR schools" can be rejected.

Association between achievement motivation and achievement in mathematics of the students of APSWR schools

The present study is intended to identify whether there exists any association between achievement motivation and achievement in mathematics of the students of APSWR schools. For this, the values of Pearson product moment[7] were computed by which the association among these two areas will be identified. Pearson's product moment method of calculating correlation coefficient (r) was chosen as it is the most appropriate technique among all the techniques.

"Because most educational data are expressed in continuous scores, this is the most frequently used correlational technique. The product moment correlation is subject to a smaller standard error than the other techniques." [8] The product moment correlation[9] is said to be the most often used and most precise coefficient of correlation, the most widely used to measure the relationship between the variables and the one most commonly computed[10]. To determine the significance of the magnitude 'r' Cohen and Holliday's table was referred to[11]. The statistical data and their results are given below.

Hypothesis 3

"There is a significant association between achievement motivation and achievement in mathematics in APSWR school students."

To test the validity of hypothesis 3, the Pearson ' r ' value was computed.

Table 4.19

Association in the whole sample (Pearson ' r ' value)

Sample size	Achievement Motivation with Achievement in Mathematics
480	0.09*

df=n - 2 = 478   ** Not significant at 0.01 level.*

ρ at 0.01 level is 0.115

The calculated value 0.09 is less than the value in the table at 0.01 level (r = 0.115), which denotes that there is no significant association between achievement motivation and achievement in mathematics.

The hypothesis that "there is a significant association between achievement motivation and achievement in mathematics in APSWR school students" can be rejected.

Hypothesis 3A

"There is a significant association between achievement motivation and achievement in mathematics of boys and girls of APSWR schools."

The association between achievement in motivation and achievement in mathematics of boys and girls is tried in the following way.

Table 4.20

Association in boys and girls (Pearson ' r ' value)

Variable	Sample size	Achievement Motivation with Achievement in Mathematics
Boys	240	0.07*
Girls	240	0.07*

df=238 * *Not significant at 0.01 level*

ρ at 0.01 level is 0.181

From the table 4.20, the Pearson ' r ' value indicated the associationship between boys and girls was same, and it was at the negligible level. Here, the calculated value 0.07 is less than the value in the table at 0.01 level (r = 0.181) and hence it is not significant.

The hypothesis that "there is a significant association between achievement motivation and achievement in mathematics of boys and girls of APSWR schools" can be rejected.

Hypothesis 3B

"There is a significant association between achievement motivation and achievement in mathematics of the students of rural and urban APSWR schools."

To test the validity of the hypothesis 3B, the Pearson ' r ' values were computed.

Table 4.21

Association in the students of rural and urban APSWR schools (Pearson ' r ' value)

Variable	Sample size	Achievement Motivation with Achievement in Mathematics
Rural	240	0.04*
Urban	240	0.13*

df=238 ** Not significant at 0.01 level.*

ρ at 0.01 level is 0.181

From the table 4.21, the Pearson ' r ' value indicated that the association between rural and urban APSWR school students was very low. The calculated value 0.04 or 0.13 is less than the value in the table at the 0.01 level (r = 0.181) and hence it is not significant.

The hypothesis that "there is a significant association between achievement motivation and achievement in mathematics of the students of rural and urban APSWR schools" can be rejected.

Hypothesis 3C

"There is a significant association between achievement motivation and achievement in mathematics of SC and OBC students of APSWR schools."

To test the validity of hypothesis 3C, the Pearson ' r ' values were computed and they are given here under.

Table 4.22

Association in the SC and OBC students (Pearson ' r ' value)

Variable	Sample size	Achievement Motivation with Achievement in Mathematics
SC	360	0.04*
OBC	120	0.34#

**df = 358, r = 0.148* — ** Not significant at 0.01 level.*

**df = 118, r = 0.228* — *# Significant at 0.01 level.*

The 'r' value from the table 4.22 indicates that there is a significant association between achievement motivation and achievement in mathematics of OBC students of APSWR schools. There is no association in SC students.

As the hypothesis that "there is a significant association between achievement motivation and achievement in mathematics of SC and OBC students of APSWR schools" cannot neither be accepted nor be rejected because of the conflicting results of table 4.22. The same hypothesis is restated in the following manner.

The Hypothesis that

"there is a significant association between achievement motivation and achievement in mathematics of SC students of APSWR schools" can be rejected.

"there is a significant association between achievement motivation and achievement in mathematics of OBC students of APSWR schools" can be accepted.

Documentation

1. Rummel J. Francis, An Introduction to Research Procedures in Education, 1958, p. 169

2. Garret E. Henry and woodworth, R.S., Statistics in Psychology and Education, 1985, pp. 112 - 114.

3. Gupta, S.P., Statistical Methods, 1980, p. E-7.4.
4. Best, J.W., Research in Education, 1982, p. 229.
5. Garret and Woodworth, op.cit., p. 215.
6. Ibid., p. 253.
7. Cohen, L. and Holliday M. Statistics for Education and Physical Education, pp. 138 - 139
8. Walter R. Borg and Meredith Damien Gall, Educational Research, 1979, p.488
9. John W. Best, Research in Education, 1982, p .247
10. George A. Fergusson, Statistical Analysis in Psychology and Education, 1981, p. 108
11. Cohen and Holliday, op.cit., p. 250

5

Summary, Conclusions and Discussion

Overview

This chapter is the final one - a fitting finale of the research report. It consists of eight sections. The first one gives an overview of the entire chapter. The second one provides an introduction to the research topic. The third section restates the problem, general objectives and hypotheses of the study for ready reference and subsequent discussion. The fourth section briefly describes of sampling design. The fifth one focusses on the establishment of instruments. The sixth section is a discussion on the findings. The seventh section lists the limitations of the study. The eighth one identifies the scope for further research in this field.

Introduction

The responsibilities of a citizen in a democracy, such as ours, are manifold and important. In public affairs, he has to make decisions, or appraise those made by fellow citizens, on local, national and international issues. In the business, as well as in economic fields also, a large portion of our activities are mathematical in nature. Mathematics is basic to a large number of branches of human knowledge. Mathematical knowledge is essential to citizenship competence. The habit of thinking can be developed through the study of mathematics. Hence, study of mathematics is very much advocated in the educational programme for the development of higher order mental capacities like critical thinking and logical reasoning.

If the students possess achievement motivation, they may be initiative, confident to the problems to be done in the class and from other books, to satisfy their deep and extensive interest. They may wish to go on doing to satisfy their intellectual hunger. The achievement motivation may also influence their regularity, their attention in the classes, their aspirations to achieve in terms of marks or solving the complex and challenging sums or puzzles, and their choice of friends based on their interest and so on. So, the investigator intended to identify the achievement motivation of students.

Mathematics is considered a necessary subject for all the learners. It demands practice and application in the daily life which is possible only when the students have achievement motivation in learning. Achievement motivation is the key factor in achieving success in any task that one performs, whatever one learns. Achievement motivation plays a dominant role in making to learn any thing. Hence, the investigator wanted to identify the level of achievement in mathematics.

The investigator was also interested in identifying the association between achievement motivation and achievement in mathematics.

The Problem

Problem

A STUDY OF THE ACHIEVEMENT MOTIVATION AND ACHIEVEMENT IN MATHEMATICS OF APSWR SCHOOL STUDENTS

Objectives

The following objectives were framed for the present research study.

1. To find out the level of achievement motivation possessed by the students of APSWR schools.
2. To find out the level of achievement in mathematics possessed by the students of APSWR schools.
3. To identify the association between achievement motivation and achievement in mathematics of APSWR schools.
4. To compare the achievement motivation and achievement in mathematics of boys and girls of APSWR schools.
5. To compare the achievement motivation and achievement in mathematics of rural and urban APSWR school students.
6. To compare the achievement motivation and achievement in mathematics of SC and OBC students of APSWR schools.
7. To find out the association between achievement motivation and achievement in mathematics in APSWR school students.
8. To find out the association between achievement motivation and achievement in mathematics of boys and girls of APSWR schools.
9. To find out the association between achievement motivation and achievement in mathematics of the students of rural and urban APSWR school students
10. To find out the association between achievement motivation and achievement in mathematics of SC and OBC students of APSWR schools.

Hypotheses

Hypothesis 1

APSWR school students are possessing high achievement motivation.

Hypothesis 1A

There is a significant difference in the level of achievement motivation possessed by boys and girls of APSWR schools.

Hypothesis 1B

There is a significant difference in the level of achievement motivation possessed by the students of rural and urban APSWR schools.

Hypothesis 1C

There is a significant difference in the level of achievement motivation possessed by SC and OBC students of APSWR schools.

Hypothesis 2

APSWR school students are possessing high achievement in mathematics

Hypothesis 2A

There is a significant difference in the level of achievement in mathematics possessed by boys and girls of APSWR schools.

Hypothesis 2B

There is a significant difference in the level of achievement in mathematics possessed by the students of rural and urban APSWR schools.

Hypothesis 2C

There is a significant difference in the level of achievement in mathematics possessed by SC and OBC students of APSWR schools.

Hypothesis 3

There is a significant association between achievement motivation and achievement in mathematics in APSWR school students.

Hypothesis 3A

There is a significant association between achievement motivation and achievement in mathematics of boys and girls of APSWR schools.

Hypothesis 3B

There is a significant association between achievement motivation and achievement in mathematics of the students of rural and urban APSWR schools.

Hypothesis 3C

There is a significant association between achievement motivation and achievement in mathematics of SC and OBC students of APSWR schools.

Sampling Design

Stratified sampling technique, after making a detailed study of different techniques of sampling, is found to be the most appropriate technique for the present study as this study involves splitting of the sample into a good number of groups according to different variables. Through stratified sampling only it is possible to divide the sample into different groups and choose students from each of these groups. Random sampling technique is also employed to select students from each group.

Regarding the size of the sample, 480 was found appropriate. This is found suitable because the study involves due intensity and detail, a sample with more than 480 students would involve a lot of resources and, the more important one, less than 480 students would also bring about problems of representativeness. Hence, 480 was considered appropriate number for the sample.

Only the students studying in Xth class in APSWR schools of third zone (south coastal) of Andhra Pradesh consists Guntur, Prakasam, Nellore districts are included in the sample. This decision is taken because the children's achievement motivation gets formed initially at the age of 14 or 15. The mathematics of Xth class decides their career at +2 stage.

A sample of 480 Xth class students was taken. Out of the total sample, 240 boys and 240 girls were selected. Out of these 240 boys or girls, 120 students from rural area APSWR schools and 120 students from urban area APSWR schools were selected. SC and OBC students were selected in the ratio of 75 : 25, as per the admission criteria followed in APSWR schools.

With the above splitting of total sample into various strata, the final sub-group sample sizes were :

Boys 240 and girls 240

Rural 240 and urban 240

SC 360 and OBC 120

Instrumentation

A research tool or instrument plays a major role in any worthwhile research, as it was the sole factor in determining the sound data and in arriving at perfect conclusions about the problem or study in hand, which ultimately, help in providing suitable remedial measures to the problem.

Using of constructed and standardized achievement motivation scale to measure the achievement motivation was one of the important methods. In the present study also, the investigator taken such achievement motivation scale which was constructed and standardized by Dr. Shah Beena of Garhwal University. There are forty partly completed sentences in this test. Each sentence can be completed meaningfully, if one links it up with any of the alternatives offered. The task is to select only one answer which seems to correspond most with one's present feelings and then put a tick mark (✓) against the selected alternative. All the items in test have to be answered. It was with a three point scale. Weightage 1, 2 and 3 are respectively awarded for alternatives (a), (b) and (c) respectively of any statement. So, the scale value lies between 40 and 120.

Marks of quarterly examination were taken to assess the achievement in mathematics.

Findings and Discussion

The following are the conclusions drawn from the analysis of data.

The APSWR school students were possessing an average level of achievement motivation. The distribution of achievement motivation is normal in the whole sample.

Bharati (1984), Tiwari (1984) and Chattergi (1983) found a high achievement motivation in their studies, which is a contradictory result from the present study.

It is the duty and obligation of the teachers to enhance the present status of achievement motivation by giving rewards and punishments, by praising and blaming, by developing competition and co-operation among students, by explaining the successes and failures of the students and their implications, by providing knowledge of results and progress of each and every student of the class, by satisfying as well as by hitting the ego of the child, by showing affection on the student, by arousing curiosity in learning, by providing security when situation demands, by fixing reasonable goals to achieve, and by following student-centered approaches in the class rooms.

It is the responsibility of the parents as well as school administration to promote achievement motivation among students in order to make them achieve well in the examinations.

The boys and girls of APSWR schools were possessing average achievement motivation without any significant difference between them.

This result is supporting the studies of Bharati (1984), Sinha (1986), Lalitha (1982) and Ahluwalia (1985).

As there is no significant difference in achievement motivation of boys and girls, it is the responsibility of the teachers and parents to inculcate and promote better achievement motivation in boys and girls in order to make them compete equally in every academic endeavour.

The rural and urban students were holding an average achievement motivation without any significant difference between them.

The study of Ahluwalia (1985) is in support of the present study.

Because of the environment and the facilities available in rural and urban areas, it is supposed to be a difference in achievement motivation between these two types of students. But, as the present study did not find any significant difference in their achievement motivation, it would be better and useful if the samples are provided with necessary guidance to enhance their achievement motivation in order to choose and study different challenging courses without worrying much about the rural and urban backgrounds.

The SC and OBC students were possessing an average achievement motivation without any significant difference between them.

The parents and the school community are supposed to help the SC as well as OBC students in cultivating and promoting achievement motivation.

The APSWR school students were holding average achievement in mathematics. The distribution of achievement in Mathematics was normal in the sample.

This result is contradicting the studies of Sridevi (1984) and Bhaskara Rao and Pushpalatha (1996).

Usually, the students fail to achieve highly in mathematics and it is also seen in the present study. This result also may be due to the socio-economic status and personality of the students studying in APSWR schools.

The teachers of mathematics should help the students in achieving well in mathematics by effective teaching, remedial instruction, individual tutoring, supervised study, making them participate in mathematical quizzes and competitions, etc.

The boys and girls were with average achievement in mathematics without any significant difference between them.

The studies of Katiyar (1979), Khatoon (1988) and Chitkar (1985) are supporting the present study and the study of Sridevi (1994) is opposing the result of the present study.

The teachers, parents and the community have to provide the necessary moral support to either sex without showing any gender discrimination to support both boys and girls in achieving excellency in mathematics.

The rural and urban students were possessing average achievement in mathematics without any significant difference between them.

The findings of Bhaskar Rao and Pushpalatha (1996) and Rattaiah and Bhaskar Rao (1998) are contradicting the above result as these studies found a high achievement.

The teachers working in rural and urban schools should motivate the students and teach according to the individual differences in order to give the necessary impetus to achievement in mathematics.

The SC and OBC students were possessing average achievement in mathematics without any significant difference between them.

Though the socio-economic status of SC students differs from the OBC students, they have got the achievement in mathematics on par with OBC students. It is a good sign and hence it is the obligation of the teachers to keep up this standard of SC students. It is their obligation also in extending their fullest support to the SC students along with OBC students to achieve equally in mathematics.

There was no significant association between achievement motivation and achievement in mathematics of APSWR school students.

The finding of the present study is not in support of the findings of Mehta (1987), Rajput (1984), Vimala (1985) and Fatima (1986).

This study is not in support of the popular assumption and research studies which state a positive significant association between achievement motivation and academic achievement. So, the teachers should try to find out the reasons that are lying behind the result of the present study and should try to bring an association between these two so as to make the students excel well in achievement in mathematics.

There was no association between achievement motivation and achievement in mathematics of boys and girls.

This result is supporting the finding of Singh (1984).

The school administration and the teachers are supposed to enhance both achievement motivation and achievement in mathematics by following the procedures or methods that influence both of these.

There was no significant association between achievement motivation and achievement in mathematics of rural and urban students.

As the present study did not find any association between achievement motivation and achievement in mathematics, the teachers may try to bring an association between these two by involving the students to the core.

There was no significant association between achievement motivation and achievement in Mathematics of SC and OBC students.

The teachers as well as the administration of APSWR schools should take necessary steps to enhance the status of achievement motivation and achievement in mathematics by which a positive and significant correlation may be brought.

Limitations of the Study

The present study was limited to the following because of the availability of time and resources.

1. The present study was confined to the study of achievement motivation and achievement in mathematics of APSWR schools without taking any sample from other schools.

2. This study did not consider the socio-economic status and psychological variables.

3. This study did not study the school environment and its influence on achievement motivation and achievement in mathematics.

4. This study did not consider the influence of study habits, academic and vocational interests on achievement motivation and achievement in mathematics.

5. This study did not consider the influence of parental background and the teachers personality on the achievement motivation and achievement in mathematics.

6. This study was confined only to third zone which includes Guntur, Prakasam and Nellore districts of Andhra Pradesh.

Scope for Further Research

The present study brings to light a good number of new areas to be studied by the future researchers. The areas and variables which are not covered by this study may be put to test to enlighten the factors associated with the inculcation and development of achievement motivation and enhancement of achievement in mathematics. So, the researchers may think of the following areas to study in detail.

1. Studies on achievement motivation may be extended to the other educational levels, viz, primary and college levels at district and state levels.

2. Studies on achievement motivation may be extended to Navodaya, Kendriya, APTWR, APR and Army schools.

3. Studies may be taken up to find out the effect of independent variables on dependent variables in the cases of controlled and experimental groups as this study has not used any special controlled variables.

4. Studies may be conducted to find out the effect of environmental and psychological factors on the inculcation and development of achievement motivation.

5. Studies on the influence of teaching community may be taken up as this factor has a great role to play in the development of achievement motivation.

6. Studies may be taken up to identify the reasons for the possession of average achievement motivation as found in this study.

7. Studies may be conducted on the use of audio-visual teaching aids, laboratory and library facilities in the schools as these have greater influence on achievement motivation.

Bibliography

Aggarwal, J.C. (1995). *Theory and Principles of Education.* New Delhi: Vikas Publishing House Pvt. Ltd.

Aggarwal, S. M. (1987). *A Course in Teaching of Modern Mathematics.* Delhi : Dhanpat Rai & Sons.

Ary, D., Jacobs, L. C. and Razavieth, A. (1972). *Introduction of Research in Education.* New York : Holt, Rinehart and Winston.

Best, J. W. (1982). *Research in Education.* New Delhi : Prentice Hall.

Bhaskara Rao, D. (1995). *Scientific Aptitude.* New Delhi : Ashish Publishers House.

Bhaskara Rao, D. (1996). *Scientific Attitude Vis-A-Vis Scientific Aptitude.* New Delhi : Discovery Publishing House.

Bhaskara Rao, D, and Puspalatha. D., (1995). *Achievement in Mathematics.* New Delhi : Discovery Publishing House.

Buch, M. B., Chief Editor. (1987). *Third Survey of Research in Education, 1978-1983.* New Delhi : National Council of Educational Research and Training.

Buch, M. B., Chief Editor. (1991). *Fourth Survey of Research in Education, 1983-1988.* New Delhi : National Council of Educational Research and Training.

Sharma, A. K., Chairman, Editorial Board. (1997). *Fifth Survey of*

Educational Research, 1988-1992. New Delhi : National Council of Educational Research and Training.

Bhatia, H. R. (1965). *A Textbook of Educational Psychology*. Bombay: Asia Publishing House.

Bhatia, K. K. (1996). *Principles of Education*. Ludhiana : Kalyani Publishers.

Chauhan, S. S. (1978). *Advanced Educational Psychology*. New Delhi: Vikas Publishing Pvt. Ltd.

Dewal, O. S. (1999). *A Handbook on Educational Research*. New Delhi : National Council for Teacher Education.

Elhance, D. N. (1973). *Fundamentals of Statistics*. Allahabad : Kitab Mahal.

Ferguson, G. A. (1981). *Statistical Analysis in Psychology and Education*. Auckland : Mc Graw Hill.

Garret, E. H. (1985). *Statistics in Psychology and Education*. Bombay : Vakils, Feffer and Simons Ltd.

Guilford, J. P. and Benjamin, F. (1973). *Fundamental Statistics in Psychology and Education*. Tokyo : Mc Graw Hill.

Herbert, J. W. and Geneva, D. H., Editors-in-Chief. (1990). *International Encyclopedia of Educational Evaluation*. New York : Pergamon Press.

Husen, T. and Poshelthwaite, T. N., Editors-in-Chief. (1985). *The International Encyclopedia of Education*. New York : Pergamon Prev.

John Babu, Ch., Rajendra Prasad, T. J., Madhukar, G. H. and Bhaskara Rao, D. (2001). *Problem Solving in Mathematics*. New Delhi : A. P. H. Publishing Corporation.

John, W. (1984). *The Aims of Education Restated*. London : Routledge and Kegan Paul.

Kamala, B. and Bhatia, B. D. (1997). *Theory and Principles of Education*. New Delhi : Doaba House.

Kamat, A. R. (1985). *Educational and Social Change in India*. Bombay: Somaiya Publications Pvt. Ltd.

Kuppuswamy, B. (1964). *Advanced Educational Psychology*. New Delhi: University Publishers.

Louis, C. and Michael, H. (1979). *Statistics for Education and Physical Education*. London : Harper & Row Publishers.

Mangal, S. K. (1993). *Advanced Educational Psychology*. New Delhi : Prentice-Hall of India Pvt. Ltd.

Mangal, S. K. (1998). *Educational Psychology*. Ludhiana : Prakash Brothers.

Merlin, C. W., Chief Editor. (1986). *Handbook of Research on Teaching*. A Project of the American Educational Research Association, New York : MacMillan Publishing Company.

Morris, L. B. and Mourice, P. H. (1980). *Psychological Foundations of Education*. New York : Harper & Row Publishers.

Papalia, D. E. and Sally, W. O. (1987). *Psychology*. New York : McGraw-Hill Book Company.

Petrovsky, A. V. and Yarosheusky, M. G. (1985). *A Concise Psychological Dictionary*. Moscow : Progress Publishers.

Pillai, J. K. (1999). *Effective Teaching*. Madurai : Madurai Kamaraj University.

Philosophy of Education. (1998). *M. Ed., Study Material*. Tiruchirapalli : Bharathidasan University.

Rai, B. C. (1981). *Method Teaching of Mathematics*. Lucknow : Prakash Kendra.

Richard, W. C. (1979). *How Children Learn Mathematics*. New York : MacMillan Publishing Company Inc.

Rummel, J. Francis. (1958). *An Introduction to Research Procedures in Education*. New York : Harper and Brothers.

Seetharamu, A. S. (1989). *Philosophies of Education*. New Delhi : Ashish Publishing House.

Shakuntaladevi. (1987). *More Puzzles to Puzzle you*. New Delhi : Orient Paperbacks.

Sidhu, K. S. (1999). *The Teaching of Mathematics*. New Delhi : Sterling Publishers Pvt. Ltd.

Skinner, C. E. (1984). *Educational Psychology*. New Delhi : Prentice Hall of India Pvt. Ltd.

Soujanya, C. M. (2000). *A Study of the Relationship Between Mathematical Internet and Academic Achievement in Mathematics of IX class pupils in Guntur City*. Unpublished Master of Education Dissertation, Nagarjuna University, Nagarjuna Nagar.

Sodhi, T. S., Sandhu, G S. and Balwant, S. S. (1988). *Philosophies of Education*. Ambala Cantt : The Indian Publications.

Sridevi, C. (1991). *A Comparative Study of the Achievement in Mathematics and Educational Aspirations of Intermediate Students Studying in Residential and Non-residential Junior Colleges*. Unpublished Master of Education Dissertation, Nagarjuna University, Nagarjuna Nagar.

Walter, R. B. and Meredith, D. G. (1979). *Educational Research*. New York : Longman.

Additional Reading

Bhaskara Rao, Digumarti (1994). *Scientific Aptitude*. New Delhi: Ashish Publishing House.

Bhaskara Rao, Digumarti (1995). *Animal Kingdom*. New Delhi: Discovery Publishing House.

Bhaskara Rao, Digumarti (1995). *Batracology*. New Delhi: Discovery Publishing House.

Bhaskara Rao, Digumarti (1996). *Scientific Attitude vis-à-vis Scientific Aptitude*. New Delhi: Discovery Publishing House.

Bhaskara Rao, Digumarti, editor (1996). *Encyclopaedia of Education For All*, 5 Vols. New Delhi: APH Publishing Corporation.

Vol. I Education For All: The World Conference.

Vol. II Education For All: The EPA-9 Summit.

Vol. III Education For All: Quality Education For All.

Vol. IV Education For All: Planning and Monitoring.

Vol. V Education For All: The Indian Scenario

Bhaskara Rao, Digumarti, Editor (1996). *Global Perceptions on Peace Education*, 3 Vols. New Delhi: Discovery Publishing House.

Bhaskara Rao, Digumarti, Editor (1996). *National Policy on Education*, 2 Vols. New Delhi: Anmol Publications Pvt. Ltd.

Bhaskara Rao, Digumarti, Editor (1997). *Care the Child*, 2 Vols. New Delhi: Discovery Publishing House.

Bhaskara Rao, Digumarti, Editor (1997) *Education for the 21st Century*, New Delhi: Discovery Publishing House.

Bhaskara Rao, Digumarti, Editor (1997). *Reflections on Scientific Attitude*. New Delhi: Discovery Publishing House.

Bhaskara Rao, Digumarti, Editor (1997). *Scientific Attitude*. New Delhi: Discovery Publishing House.

Bhaskara Rao, Digumarti, Editor (1997). *Success Story of a Primary Education Project*. New Delhi: APH Publishing Corporation.

Bhaskara Rao, Digumarti, Editor (1997). *World Food Summit*, 3 Vols. New Delhi: Discovery Publishing House.

Bhaskara Rao, Digumarti, Editor (1998). *Adolescence Education*. New Delhi: Discovery Publishing House.

Bhaskara Rao, Digumarti, Editor (1998). *Community and School Nutrition Education*. New Delhi: Discovery Publishing House.

Bhaskara Rao, Digumarti, Editor (1998). *District Primary Education Programme*. New Delhi: Discovery Publishing House.

Bhaskara Rao, Digumarti, Editor (1998). *Earth Summit*. 2 Vols. New Delhi: Discovery Publishing House.

Bhaskara Rao, Digumarti, Editor (1998). *National Policy on Education: Towards An Enlightened and Humane Society*, New Delhi: Discovery Publishing House.

Bhaskara Rao, Digumarti, Editor (1998). *Reforming School Education*. New Delhi: Discovery Publishing House.

Bhaskara Rao, Digumarti, Editor (1998). *Teacher Education in India*. New Delhi: Discovery Publishing House.

Bhaskara Rao, Digumarti, Editor (1998). *World Summit for Social Development*. New Delhi: Discovery Publishing House.

Bhaskara Rao, Digumarti, Editor (2000). *Education For All: Achieving the Goal*, 3 Vols. New Delhi: APH Publishing Corporation.

Vol. I The Global Consensus.

Vol. II Mid-Decade Review Reports of Regional Seminars.

Vol. III Issues and Trends.

Bhaskara Rao, Digumarti, Editor (2000), *International Encyclopaedia of AIDS*, 11 Vols. in 13 parts. New Delhi: Discovery Publishing House.

Vol. 1 Introduction to HIV/AIDS.

Vol. 2 HIV/AIDS—Issues and Challenges, 2 parts.

Vol. 3 HIV/AIDS—Socio Economic Realities.

Vol. 4 HIV/AIDS—Law Ethics and Human Rights, 2 parts.

Vol. 5 AIDS and NGOs.

Vol. 6 AIDS and Home Care.

Vol. 7 STD Case Management.

Vol. 8 HIV/AIDS Prevention and Care—Teaching Modules for Nurses and Midwives.

Vol. 9 HIV Prevention Education for Education for Educational Institutions.

Vol. 10 Instructional Modules for AIDS Education.

Vol. 11 School Health Education to Prevent AIDS and STD—A Package for Curriculum Planners.

Bhaskara Rao, Digumarti, Editor (2000). *Global Synthesis of Educational Achievement*. New Delhi: Discovery Publishing House.

Bhaskara Rao, Digumarti, Editor (2000). *International Encyclopaedia Science and Technology Education,* 10 Vols. New Delhi: Discovery Publishing House.

Vol. 1 Science and Technology Education.

Vol. 2 Science Education in Developing Countries.

Vol. 3 Organisational Structure of Science.

Vol. 4 Science Education in Asia and the Pacific.

Vol. 5 Science and Technology Education for All.

Vol. 6 Values, Ethics, Talent and Girls in Science and Technology Education.

Vol. 7 Popularization of Science and Technology Education.

Vol. 8 Science, Power and Society.

Vol. 9 Information Technology.

Vol. 10 Teacher Training in Science and Technology: A Curriculum Framework.

Bhaskara Rao, Digumarti, Editor (2001). *Distance Education in Different Countries*. New Delhi: APH Publishing Corporation.

Bhaskara Rao, Digumarti, Editor (2001). *Decentralised Management of Education (Management of Education in Panchayati Raj and Municipal Bodies)*. New Delhi: Discovery Publishing House.

Bhaskara Rao, Digumarti, Editor (2001). *Electrochemistry for Environmental Protection*. New Delhi: Discovery Publishing Corporation.

Bhaskara Rao, Digumarti, Editor (2001). *Global Educational Studies*. New Delhi: Discovery Publishing House.

Bhaskara Rao, Digumarti, Editor (2001). *International Encyclopaedia of Human Rights*, 7 Vols. in 13 Parts. New Delhi: Discovery Publishing House.

Vol. 1 International Instruments of Human Rights, 2 parts.

Vol. 2 Regional Instruments of Human Rights, 2 parts.

Vol. 3 Human Rights and the United Nations, 2 parts.

Vol. 4 Fact Files of Human Rights, 3 parts.

Vol. 5 Study Stories of Human Rights, 3 parts.

Vol. 6 International Meetings on Human Rights, 2 parts.

Vol. 7 Professional Training in Human Rights.

Bhaskara Rao, Digumarti, Editor (2001). *Jomtein Decade of Education*. New Delhi: Discovery Publishing House.

Bhaskara Rao, Digumarti, Editor (2001). *Nuclear Materials: Issues and Concerns*, 2 Vols. New Delhi: Discovery Publishing House.

Bhaskara Rao, Digumarti, Editor (2001). *World Conference on Education for All*. New Delhi: APH Publishing Corporation.

Bhaskara Rao, Digumarti, Editor (2001). *World Conference on Human Education*. New Delhi: Discovery Publishing House.

Bhaskara Rao, Digumarti, Editor (2001). *World Conference on Science*. New Delhi: Discovery Publishing House.

Bhaskara Rao, Digumarti, Editor (2004). *Chernobyl: Never Again*. New Delhi: Discovery Publishing House.

Bhaskara Rao, Digumarti, Editor (2004). *Habitat Agenda*. New Delhi: Discovery Publishing House.

Bhaskara Rao, Digumarti, Editor, (2003). *Inspiring Experiences in Teacher Education*. New Delhi: Discovery Publishing House.

Bhaskara Rao, Digumarti, Editor (2003). *International Studies in Education*, 3 Vols. New Delhi: Discovery Publishing House.

Bhaskara Rao, Digumarti, Editor (2003). *Military Conversion: Impact on Science and Technology*. New Delhi: Discovery Publishing House.

Bhaskara Rao, Digumarti, Editor (2004). *Virology and Immunology*. New Delhi: Discovery Publishing House.

Bhaskara Rao, Digumarti, Editor (2003). *United Nations Millennium Summit*. New Delhi: Discovery Publishing House.

Bhaskara Rao, Digumarti, Editor (2003). *World Assembly on Aging*. New Delhi: Discovery Publishing House.

Bhaskara Rao, Digumarti, Editor (2003). *World Conference on Human Rights*. New Delhi: Discovery Publishing House.

Bhaskara Rao, Digumarti, Editor (2003). *World Education Forum*. New Delhi: Discovery Publishing House.

Bhaskara Rao, Digumarti, Editor (2003). *Education Employment and Human Resource Development*. New Delhi: Discovery Publishing House.

Bhaskara Rao, Digumarti, Editor (2004). *Learning to Live Together*, 3 Volumes, New Delhi: Discovery Publishing House.

Bhaskara Rao, Digumarti, Editor (2004). *Successful Schooling*. New Delhi: Discovery Publishing House.

Bhaskara Rao, Digumarti, Editor (2004). *European Education and Teachers*. New Delhi: Discovery Publishing House.

Bhaskara Rao, Digumarti, Editor (2004). *Higher Education in the 21st Century: Vision and Action*. New Delhi: Discovery Publishing House.

Bhaskara Rao, Digumarti, Editor (2004). *Teachers in a Changing World*. New Delhi: Discovery Publishing House.

Bhaskara Rao, Digumarti, C.A.P. Swamy and B.S.V. Dutt (1997). *Self Evaluation in Student Teaching*. New Delhi: Discovery Publishing House.

Bhaskara Rao, Digumarti and Digumarti Pushpa Latha (1994). *Achievement in Biology*. New Delhi: Discovery Publishing.

Bhaskara Rao, Digumarti, C. Sridevi and K. Vijaya (1995) *Achievement in Social Studies*. New Delhi: Discovery Publishing House.

Bhaskara Rao, Digumarti and Digumarti Pushpa Latha (1995). *Achievement in English*. New Delhi: Discovery Publishing.

Bhaskara Rao, Digumarti and Digumarti Pushpa Latha (1994). *Achievement in Science*. New Delhi: Discovery Publishing House.

Bhaskara Rao, Digumarti and Digumarti Pushpa Latha (1995). *Achievement in Mathematics*. New Delhi: Discovery Publishing House.

Bhaskara Rao, Digumarti and Digumarti Pushpa Latha, Editors (1998). *International Encyclopaedia of Women*, 5 Volumes. New Delhi: Discovery Publishing House.

Vol. 1 Status of World's Women.

Vol. 2 Women, Education and Empowerment.

Vol. 3 Women Challenges and Advancement.

Vol. 4 Women and Family Health.

Vol. 5 Women and International Action.

Bhaskara Rao, Digumarti, Digumarti Pushpa Latha and Digumarti Harshitha, Editors (2001). *Biological Welfare*. New Delhi: Discovery Publishing House.

Bhaskara Rao, Digumarti, Digumarti Pushpa Latha and Digumarti Harshitha, Editors (2001), *Women as Educators*. New Delhi: Discovery Publishing House.

Bhaskara Rao, Digumarti and Digumarti Harshitha, Editors (2001). *Education in India*. New Delhi: APH Publishing Corporation.

Bhaskara Rao, Digumarti, Digumarti Pushpa Latha and Digumarti Harshitha, Editors (2001). *Assessing Learning Achievement*. New Delhi: Discovery Publishing House.

Bhaskara Rao, Digumarti, Digumarti Pushpa Latha and Digumarti Harshitha, Editors (2001). *Energy Security*. New Delhi: Discovery Publishing House.

Bhaskara Rao, Digumarti, D. Harshitha and K.R.S.S. Rao, Editors (1999). *Advanced Biotechnology*. New Delhi: Discovery Publishing House.

Bhaskara Rao, Digumarti and D. Sridhar (2002). *Job Satisfaction of School Teachers*. New Delhi: Discovery Publishing House.

Bhaskara Rao, Digumarti and K.R.S. Sambasiva Rao, Editors (1996). *Current Trends in Indian Education*. New Delhi: Discovery Publishing House.

Bhaskara Rao, Digumarti and K. Vijaya (1995). *A Text Book Evaluation*. Ambala Cantt: The Associated Publishers.

Bhaskara Rao, Digumarti and N.V.M. Mohana Rao (2002). *Problems of Mentally Handicapped Children*. New Delhi: Discovery Publishing House.

Bhaskara Rao, Digumarti, V.V. Rao, V.V. Lakshmi and V.V. Krishna, Editors (1999). *Status and Advancement of Women*. New Delhi: APH Publishing Corporation.

Babu, P.C. and Digumarti Bhaskara Rao, Editor (2003). *Flowers of Wisdom*. New Delhi: Discovery Publishing House.

Bhagya Lakshmi, Lingineni, and Digumarti Bhaskara Rao, Editor (2000). *Reading and Comprehension*. New Delhi: Discovery Publishing House.

Bhuvaneswara Lakshmi, G. and Digumarti Bhaskara Rao, Editor (2000). *Attitude Towards Science*. New Delhi: Discovery Publishing House.

Devraj, T.A.S. and Digumarti Bhaskara Rao, Editor (1997). *Trace Analysis of Uranium and Thorium*. New Delhi: Discovery Publishing House.

Durga Rani, K. and Digumarti Bhaskara Rao, Editor (2000). *Educational Aspirations and Scientific Attitudes*. New Delhi: Discovery Publishing House.

Dutt, B.S.V. and Digumarti Bhaskara Rao (2001). *Empowering Primary Teachers*. New Delhi: Discovery Publishing House.

Ediger, Marlow and Digumarti Bhaskara Rao (1996). *Science Curriculum*. New Delhi: Discovery Publishing House.

Ediger, Marlow and Digumarti Bhaskara Rao (2000). *Teaching Mathematics Successfully*. New Delhi: Discovery Publishing House.

Ediger, Marlow and Digumarti Bhaskara Rao (2000). *Teaching Reading Successfully*. New Delhi: Discovery Publishing House.

Ediger, Marlow and Digumarti Bhaskara Rao (2001). *Teaching Science Successfully*. New Delhi: Discovery Publishing House.

Ediger, Marlow and Digumarti Bhaskara Rao (2001). *Teaching Social Studies Successfully*. New Delhi: Discovery Publishing House.

Ediger, Marlow and Digumarti Bhaskara Rao (2002). *Philosophy and Curriculum*. New Delhi: Discovery Publishing House.

Ediger, Marlow and Digumarti Bhaskara Rao (2002). *Improving School Administration*. New Delhi: Discovery Publishing House.

Ediger, Marlow and Digumarti Bhaskara Rao (2003). *Elementary Curriculum*. New Delhi: Discovery Publishing House.

Ediger, Marlow and Digumarti Bhaskara Rao (2003). *Language Arts Curriculum*. New Delhi: Discovery Publishing House.

Ediger, Marlow and Digumarti Bhaskara Rao (2004). *Teaching Language Arts Successfully*. New Delhi: Discovery Publishing House.

Ediger, Marlow and Digumarti Bhaskara Rao (2004). *Teaching Mathematics in Elementary Schools*. New Delhi: Discovery Publishing House.

Ediger, Marlow and Digumarti Bhaskara Rao (2004). *Teaching Science in Elementary Schools*. New Delhi: Discovery Publishing House.

Ediger, Marlow and Digumarti Bhaskara Rao (2004). *Teaching Social Studies in Elementary Schools*. New Delhi: Discovery Publishing House.

Jayasree, Kandi and Digumarti Bhaskara Rao, Editor (1999). *Correlates of Socialisation*. New Delhi: Discovery Publishing House.

John Babu, Ch. and T.J.R. Prasad, G.M. Madhukar and Digumarti Bhaskara Rao, Editors (1996). *Problems Solving in Mathematics*. New Delhi: APH Publishing Corporation.

Jyothi, Nirmala and Digumarti Bhaskara Rao, Editor (2003). *Non-detention System in School Education*. New Delhi: Discovery Publishing House.

Marja, Talvi and Digumarti Bhaskara Rao, Editors (1996). *Educational Leadership and Social Changes*. New Delhi: Discovery Publishing House.

Prabhakaram. K.S and Digumarti Bhaskara Rao, Editor (1998). *Concept Attainment Model in Mathematics Teaching*. New Delhi: Discovery Publishing House.

Prasanth Kumar, J. and Digumarti Bhaskara Rao, Editor (1998). *Effectiveness of Distance Education System*. New Delhi: Discovery Publishing House.

Prasanth Kumar, J and Digumarti Bhaskara Rao and G. Sundar Rao, Editors (2000). *Open University Student Support Services*. New Delhi: Discovery Publishing House.

Ramatulasamma, K. and Digumarti Bhaskara Rao, editor (2002). *Job Satisfaction of Teacher Educators*. New Delhi: Discovery Publishing House.

Rama Krishnaiah, D. and Digumarti Bhaskara Rao, Editor (1998). *Job Satisfaction of College Teachers*. New Delhi: Discovery Publishing House.

Rathaiah, Lavu and Digumarti Bhaskara Rao, Editors (1996). *International Innovations in Education*. New Delhi: Discovery Publishing House.

Rathaiah, Lavu and Digumarti Bhaskara Rao (1997). *Achievement Correlates*. New Delhi: Discovery Publishing House.

Ramesh, Ganta and Digumarti Bhaskara Rao, Editors (1998). *Environmental Education: Problem and Prospects*: New Delhi: Discovery Publishing House.

Reddy, Sudhakar and Digumarti Bhaskara Rao, Editor (2003). *Creativity in Adolescents*. New Delhi: Discovery Publishing House.

Reddy, M.S. and Digumarti Bhaskara Rao, Editor (2004) *Creativity in College Students*. New Delhi: Discovery Publishing House.

Rudramamba, B. and Digumarti Bhaskara Rao, Editor (2004). *Impact of the Problems of Teachers on Achievement of Pupils*. New Delhi: Discovery Publishing House.

Sanjeeva Rao, P.C. and Digumarti Bhaskara Rao, Editor (1996). *A Text Book of Geology*. New Delhi: Discovery Publishing House.

Satya Narayana, V. and Digumarti Bhaskara Rao, Editor (2001). *Physical Education, Social Attitudes and Leadership Qualities*. New Delhi: Discovery Publishing House.

Srinivasulu Reddy, M., K.R.S. Sambasiva Rao and Digumarti Bhaskara Rao, Editor (1999). *A Text Book of Aquaculture*. New Delhi: Discovery Publishing House.

Vanaja, M. and Digumarti Bhaskara Rao, Editor (1999). *Inquiry Training Model*. New Delhi: Discovery Publishing House.

Valeri V. Koustiouk and Digumarti Bhaskara Rao, Editor (2002). *A Text Book of Crygenics*. New Delhi: Discovery Publishing House

Valeri V. Koustiouk and Digumarti Bhaskara Rao, Editor (2004). *Refrigiration and Environment*. New Delhi: Discovery Publishing House.

Veen Kumari, Balusu and Digumarti Bhaskara Rao, Editor (1996). *Operation Black Board*. New Delhi: Discovery Publishing House.

Veena Kumari, B. and Digumarti Bhaskara Rao, Editor (2000). *Psycho-Social Correlates of Achievement*. New Delhi: Discovery Publishing House.

Venkata Rao, P. and Digumarti Bhaskara Rao (1989). *A Text Book of Zoology—Junior Intermediate*. Guntur: Vignan Publishers.

Venkata Rao, P. and Digumarti Bhaskara Rao (1989). *A Text Book of Zoology—Senior Intermediate*. Guntur: Vignan Publishers.

Venugopala Rao, K. and Digumarti Bhaskara Rao, Editor (2000). *Teacher Morale in Secondary Schools*. New Delhi: Discovery Publishing House.

Vidya, C. and Digumarti Bhaskara Rao, Editor (1996). *A Text Book of Nutrition*. New Delhi: Discovery Publishing House.

Vidya Bharathi, D. and Digumarti Bhaskara Rao, Editor (2000). *Educational Philosophies of Swami Vivekanand and John Dewey*. New Delhi: APH Publishing Corporation.

Vidya, C. and Digumarti Bhaskara Rao, Editor (1996). *A Text Book of Nutrition*. New Delhi: Discovery Publishing House.

Bhaskara Rao, Digumarti (1986). *Dhrushya Sravana Bodhanapakaranalu* (Audio Visual Teaching Aids) Guntur: Nagarjuna Publishers.

Bhaskara Rao, Digumarti (1993). *Jeevasashtra Bodhana* (Teaching of Biology). Guntur: Nagarjuna Publishers.

Bhaskara Rao, Digumarti (1995). *Vignanasasthra Bodhana* (Teaching of Science) Guntur: Nagarjuna Publishers.

Bhaskara Rao, Digumarti (1997). *Vidya Manovigana Seshtram* (Educational Psychology) Guntur: Creative Press.

Bhaskara Rao, Digumarti (1998). *DSC Study Material*. Guntur: Nagarjuna Publishers.

Bhaskara Rao, Digumarti (1998). *Upadhyayudu Vidya* (Teacher and Education). Guntur: Nagarjuna Publishers.

Bhaskara Rao, Digumarti (1998). *Vidya Drukpadalu* (Perspectives of Education). Guntur: Nagarjuna Publishers.

Bhaskara Rao, Digumarti (1999). *EdCET Teaching Aptitude*. Guntur: Nagarjuna Publishers.

Bhaskara Rao, Digumarti (2001). *Bharata Samajamulo Upadyayudu Vidya* (Teacher and Education in Emerging Indian Society). Guntur: Nagarjuna Publishers.

Bhaskara Rao, Digumarti (2001). *Bhoutika Sastra Bodhana Paddathulu* (Methods of Teaching Physical Science). Guntur: Nagarjuna Publishers.

Bhaskara Rao, Digumarti (2001). *Jeeva Sastra Bodhana Padhathulu* (Methods of Teaching Biology). Guntur: Nagarjuna Publishers.

Bhaskara Rao, Digumarti (2001). *Vidya Manovignana Sastram* (Educational Psychology). Guntur: Nagarjuna Publishers.

Bhaskara Rao, Digumarti (2003). *Patasala Yajamanyam Paripalana* (School Management and Administration). Guntur Nagarjuna Publishers.

Bhaskara Rao, Digumarti (2003). *Vidya Sanketika Sastram Mariyu Computer Vidya* (Educational Technology and Computer Education). Guntur: Nagarjuna Publishers.

Index